SO-CAD-579

THE STATE OF
BLACK
AMERICA
2001

PUBLISHED BY NATIONAL URBAN LEAGUE ⊜

The State of Black America 2001

EDITOR
Lee A. Daniels

ASSOCIATE EDITORS
Dachell McSween
William I. Dawson

MANAGING EDITOR
Hollie I. West

DEPUTY MANAGING EDITOR
Rose Jefferson-Frazier

IMAGE PARTNERS
CUSTOM PUBLISHING

PRESIDENT AND
CREATIVE DIRECTOR
John Shearer

VICE PRESIDENT
Marianne Shearer

DESIGN DIRECTOR
Lisa Weber

ART DIRECTOR
Roger B. Weisman

Copyright© National Urban League, 2001
Library of Congress Catalog Number 77-647469
ISBN 0-914758-91-8
$24.95

NATIONAL URBAN LEAGUE

Our Children ⊜ *Our Destiny*

Cover Image by
John Shearer

TABLE OF CONTENTS

TABLE OF CONTENTS

It's Our Responsibility. It's Their Turn

LEE A. DANIELS

N ow, as the twenty-first century opens, we're being bombarded with implicit and explicit declarations that race—which is to say the pressing by African Americans of issues from a racial perspective—is *passé*.

It is said: *Racism is no longer a significant factor affecting the lives of African Americans. It's a matter of "class" now.*

It is said: *And, why, look at the advances Asian Americans and Latino Americans have made. They don't*—and here that ugly coded phrase is wielded—*play the race card.*

It is said: *The new generation of African Americans, all those young blacks who've come of age in the 1980s and 1990s. For them, the Civil Rights Movement is, not lived experience, but history. They see things differently. Once they take over, race will come to mean less.*

And so on.

Well, the rap group Public Enemy had a notion that is a fit response to this dynamic of denial: Don't believe the hype.

That black people of today, no matter what their station, do not believe the hype has been apparent all through the last decade. Check out the congressional and presidential elections, for starters, and then move on to the black response to police racial profiling, and then ... get the picture?

Black Americans are "optimistic," but "on edge;" and "on edge but optimistic," as Hugh B. Price wrote in a June 2000 *To Be Equal* column discussing the New York Urban League's seminal survey of black New Yorkers released that month.

In fact, that survey, which was conducted by the research firm of Blum & Weprin Associates, Inc., is one piece of the voluminous evidence showing that African Americans remain highly race-conscious. It's so important that we present it in this volume with an extended analysis by Professor Walter S. Stafford, of New York University.

And we have paired that survey with a national survey (also conducted by Blum & Weprin), done for us at National Urban League headquarters specifically for this volume of *The State of Black America* that sought the views of the under-35 cohort of African Americans.

Some of the things we found, set forth in a second essay by Professor Stafford, will surprise many—and disconcert those who've been declaring the existence of a "class gap" and a "generation gap" dividing and splintering blacks in America. For example, the findings of the national survey destroy the current, ever-so-fashionable assertion that blacks who are under 35 are dismissive of affirmative action. On the contrary, they match the older cohort of blacks in the vigor of their support for it, as Hugh Price discusses in more detail in this volume's Overview, which follows.

I mention it here to underscore the point that both Urban League surveys and other surveys of black opinion that Professor Stafford takes note of in his analyses prove blacks in America remain an extraordinarily unified group across such natural points of division as income, extent of education, gender, occupation and age. Indeed, both surveys show that the better educated blacks are and the greater their annual income, the more vigorously they declare that racism remains significant. Those general findings provide a clue to some of the bedrock attitudes of the under-35 cohort of black Americans, which as a group is the most advantaged group of blacks in American history.

None of this is really surprising once you think about it: the large majority of black Americans understand from the experience of their own lives, and those of their relatives, friends, neighbors, and those blacks they read about and see in the media that it is imperative to maintain a high degree of group unity.

Black people know that serious strains of racism—the violent kind that threatens our very lives; the institutional kind that systemically works to deny us opportunity; the petty kind that means *you* get followed around the store or stopped by the police—continues. Black people in America know they've never been wrong about the persistence of racism. That's not racial chauvinism. That is racial experience, born of examining the African-American and American past and present—and living it.

Changing the wrongs of the present of the Black American Experience and building a brighter future for themselves and their descendants has been the struggle waged by every generation of African Americans since the first Africans were brought to the Virginia colony settlement of Jamestown in 1619. So it has been. So it is, and will be. These two National Urban League surveys and the essays gathered for this latest edition of *The State of Black America* show that black Americans under 35 understand that responsibility very well, and are eager to share in bearing it.

Black America's Challenge: The Re-construction of Black Civil Society

BY HUGH B. PRICE

One couldn't help but notice the undertone of glee in some of the news reports and commentary last spring that announced and accompanied the census findings that the number of Latinos in the United States—native-born, recent legal immigrants, and those in the country illegally—have now surpassed the number of Americans of African descent.

Preliminary reports from the U.S. Census Bureau indicated that what has long been expected has come to pass sooner than expected: the number of people in America who have Spanish-speaking ancestry has exploded to 35.3 million, from the 22.4 million counted in 1990. The number of blacks showed a much more modest rise, to 34.7 million, from 30 million counted a decade ago.

As I wrote in a March *To Be Equal* column noting the development, one thing the explosive growth of America's Latino population shows is the continuing pull of the material and the ideal: That is, the pull of the American economy and the nation's sometimes over-the-top display of its vast material affluence, on the one hand; and the pull of the ideal of America—its promise of freedom and a society ruled by democratic processes of government.

A second insight the numerical change offers is that the multi-ethnic, multi-racial, multi-cultural character of America is going to become more and more evident and influential. Indeed, with all the recent, media-driven celebration of Hispanic culture in America, most specifically, Hispanic music stars, it may be difficult for some to recall that less than a decade ago, "multiculturalism" was largely seen as something that was bad for America and the word was used by some as an epithet. But, then, that was when it was used primarily to refer to African Americans pushing for a greater and more specific study of the African-American past in schools and colleges and their greater inclusion into the American mainstream.

Still a third point to be drawn from the rise of the Latino community is that African Americans are no longer the nation's second largest ethnic group, and we can expect that Hispanic-Americans' growing numbers will soon bring them the increased clout in the political mainstream those numbers deserve.

There are numerous insights this last development provides in and of itself (some of which will be discussed later); but for now the point is that it underscores the need for African Americans to reconstruct Black Civil Society.

Blacks' civil society, as it is with other ethnic groups, is the aggregate of all those voluntary agencies—civic, church, fraternal, self-help, and temporary ones that spring up in response to momentary need—that make up the sinews, so to speak, of African-American communal life. They're the foundation of Black America's social and political system. Needless to say, the crucial element in this network of churches and other organizations is people. Thus, it is the people who staff these organizations, the people who live in predominantly black communities, and those who have relatives who do, the people who attend black churches, be they of the storefront or megachurch variety, the people, in other words, who understand that their destiny is tied to the well-being of African Americans as a group, who must bring about this change, this reconstruction.

The prime movers of that task, those who bear the greatest responsibility for the necessary transformation of Black Civil Society will be those black Americans who are now under 35 years old. That's the motivation for this latest volume of *The State of Black America*. It is to advance the discussion about the responsibilities of the under-35 cohort of African Americans by providing at least a part of the substantive framework that discussion demands.

To advance that discussion, we've got to get to know them better. I don't mean just our own children. I mean who they are as a group: what they think about politics and religion and marriage and family, about the public schools, about AIDS, the police, about the legacy of the Civil Rights Movement, and about their own futures. That's what our national survey, conducted especially for this volume by Blum & Weprin Associates, Inc., was designed to provide answers to.

Those answers in several instances are surprising. One example has to do with rap music and hip-hop culture, a topic whose discussion within Black America is probably more intense than the discussion occurring in the larger society. One would expect that older African Americans do not think that, generally speaking, most hip-hop and rap artists are good role models for black youth. The negative response from African Americans 35 and older reach the high-70 to low-80 percentages. And yet, as Professor Walter S. Stafford points out in his incisive analysis here, 65 percent of those 18 to 24 years old said they were poor role models, too; only 25 percent said they provided positive images for youth. That "hard" finding means we can have a more focused discussion on rap, both the genre and the artists who promulgate it; for starters, I suggest the two informative essays on rap in this volume from two of our contributors who are under 35 themselves, Yvonne Bynoe and David W. Brown.

Another finding of our national survey that slays some myths while provoking further discussion is the one showing that, as Professor Stafford writes, support for affirmative action "is nearly universal among blacks"—and that includes those in the 18 to 34 age group: 84 percent say affirmative action is still needed in higher education and the workplace. The percentages for all the age groups above them are even higher, and those blacks with undergraduate and graduate degrees were even more fervent in their support of affirmative action. Professor Stafford notes that support for affirmative action among blacks remains so high because of their "pervasive perception of racial discrimination in employment." His discussion on this point is complemented by Professor Walter Allen's trenchant examination of the battle over affirmative action in higher education.

These and other essays in this volume exemplify what's as necessary today as at any time in American history: the marrying of statistical data to trenchant observation and a commitment to advance the status of African Americans. That translates to a willingness to ask the difficult questions and propose remedies to thorny problems, as Celeste Watkins has done in "A Tale of Two Classes: The Socio-Economic Divide Among Black Americans Under 35," her important consideration of the responsibility of those blacks under 35 who are doing well to figuring out ways to extend the "opportunity ladder" to those less well-off counterparts.

Figuring that out is a part of the reconstruction of Black Civil Society that is the task ahead. African Americans as an American ethnic group are at an historic turning point. They, now with a growing educated and skilled middle class, have never been in a better position in American society. But what's lacking, as Professor Martin L. Kilson, of Harvard, wrote in a memorandum to us that helped form the basis for our thinking about these issues, is most effectively marshalling the relative affluence and skills of the new black middle class to attack the problems of that 30-percent group of poor and truly impoverished blacks who need a helping hand.

This isn't to say that such efforts haven't been made. Of course they have. Black Civil Society compiled an extraordinary record of achievement against daunting odds down through the twentieth century. From countless local community organizations to the work of black churches to the founding and work of the National Association for the Advancement of Colored People and the National Urban League themselves, the work of those who staffed Black Civil Society institutions built the foundation of progress brick by brick.

But now, we must do more, do it in different ways to respond to the new fast-paced societal imperatives of technological advancement and a globalized economy. And recruit in more systemic ways blacks under 35 into the mobilization effort.

We at the Urban League have responded to this imperative in part by launching our major national education initiative, the Campaign for African-American Achievement. The campaign, funded by the Lilly Foundation, and implemented through our national network of Urban League affiliates is designed to mobilize local communities to support the high scholastic achievement of those communities' children. Because our national Campaign partners include the mammoth Congress of National Black Churches, and nearly a score of black civic organizations, we're able to call upon their chapters and affiliates at the local community level as well. In short, our Campaign offers a model of the kind of systematic linking of the black middle class and the black poor in order to extend the opportunity the former have gained access to the latter.

Make no mistake. This isn't a call for noblesse oblige. For one thing, the poor don't need condescending lectures about the value of work. They've shown in dramatic fashion that they know work is worth pursuing not only for the dollars it brings but because it also produces individual self-esteem. The precipitous decline in the black unemployment rate to record lows in the late 1990s resulted from the black poor rushing to fill the low-wage jobs at the very bottom of the occupational ladder which the long period of economic prosperity had finally made open to them. Moreover, the

17

fortunes of the black middle class are inextricably tied to those of the black poor. That old saying that if we don't all hang together, we'll surely hang separately is still apt. It applies to those African Americans who are under 35 and have trod a golden path through college and graduate school into well-paying jobs as much as it did to black Americans of previous eras.

That is something black Americans must do regardless of where the group stands in the numerical pecking order of ethnic groups. That's why the increase of the Latino population isn't the primary spur to the need for the reconstruction of Black Civil Society. Just as the changing demographics vis-à-vis other ethnic groups offer not just challenges, but opportunities, so, too, do the changing demographics within Black America—namely, the coming into its own of the younger generation. The Urban League has experienced this firsthand in recent years through the burgeoning network of National Urban League Young Professionals, one of our auxiliaries. These young adults in professional positions forged a link with the League because they realized they needed an outlet for their commitment to help more blacks do what they did: gain the educational and the technological skills that are essential to becoming and remaining competitive in an increasingly global and technological society. That's the only way the American opportunity structure must become more and more inclusive—which has always been the ultimate goal of Black Civil Society.

The National Urban League Survey: Black America's Under-35 Generation

BY WALTER W. STAFFORD

The United States is in the midst of a dramatic multifaceted transformation, one that manifests itself in society's economic, demographic, cultural, technological, and political arenas. It may take decades before the transformation is fully understood. But we can be sure that the changes will have a great effect on black Americans, particularly, those under thirty years of age—who make up half of America's black population. America's multifaceted transformation presents formidable challenges for Black America's rising generation: In order to become economically viable and effective citizens they will have to acquire more technological and conceptual skills, negotiate with a greater variety of ethnicities and cultures, and constantly absorb rapidly breaking scientific information.

The defining characteristic of the economic transformation—frequently referred to, as the "new global economy"—has seen technological advances that have solidified the integration of capital markets and quickened the restructuring of jobs and industries. From 1985 to 2000—when the effects of the transformation began to take hold—28 million jobs were created. While black joblessness declined, black unemployment rates still remained twice that of whites, and the black-white family income gap narrowed only slightly. Even more ominously for the next generation, the mean net wealth of black families compared to whites barely budged between 1983 and 2000 (Wolff, 2000).

The demographic transition, which began with the passage of the 1965 Immigration Act, has produced the most profound population changes in the country's history and altered the historical balance among the races and ethnic groups. In 1997, the estimated foreign-born population was nearly 26 million, the largest ever, and every 1 in 10 residents was born outside the United States, the highest proportion since 1930. Most of the new immigrants have been non-Europeans and reside primarily in five metropolitan areas, where they have joined resident blacks, Latinos, and Asians as the country's fastest growing groups. Whites remain the largest group in the country but are becoming more proportional with groups of color, and blacks share of the total population now trails Hispanics.[1] Regional shifts are also important. In a historic reversal of their migration patterns, blacks are leaving the North and West to return to the South, a region they once abandoned (Frey, 2001).

The cultural transformation has been stimulated in part by the demographic changes. People of color, historically barred or limited by the country's immigration laws, have brought a polyglot of cultures—some new and some reinforcing the old—to the country which has led to a growing acceptance of bilingualism and multiculturalism. Blacks have contributed to the changes with demands that institutions—notably, public schools—acknowledge their cultural traditions. They have also been at the forefront of groups of color demanding greater diversity on television, and at the center of the national debate about "rap" music and its social and cultural effects on youth and on society in general.

The technological transformation, a product of advanced computerization, has condensed time, space, and interpersonal communications. Knowledge and information have been democratized. Disparate racial, ethnic, and cultural groups have been joined through the internet—the basis of the information superhighway—into common causes. And scientific explorations have been enhanced, introducing new explanations for DNA and reducing the discovery time for diseases. The technological revolution has also created new disparities—the digital divide—which are widening the gulf between blacks and whites, particularly blacks with limited incomes. While differences in the access of black and white students to the internet remains a matter of concern, the major gap is in the access of households. Less than one quarter of the black households have internet access, compared to nearly one half of all white households (Department of Commerce, 2000).

The most noticeable aspect of the political transformation has been the continued weakening of the federal government's commitment to entitlement programs and affirmative action. Since the 1980s, there has been a narrowing of the scope of affirmative action programs, a weakening or elimination of such entitlement programs as welfare, a greater devolution of authority to state and local governments, and now an effort to use religious institutions—faith-based charities—to deliver social services. At local levels, contentious relations between black communities and the police have continued to plague race relations.

Cognizant of the historical problems and opportunities that transformations—wars, depressions, technological advancements—have had on blacks, and uncertain whether the current transformations carry the seeds of the old forms of racism, and the strains of more virulent pathologies, the National Urban League (the League) commissioned a random telephone survey by Blum and Weprin Associates of 800 households to gain a clearer perspective of blacks' views of the changes. A major reason for conducting the survey was to expand the League's knowledge about the issues and concerns of younger blacks.

The survey questions overlapped or replicated many of the questions on other national instruments. However, the League developed a number of new questions to: (1) reflect the issues identified in their analysis of the five chief facets of the broad transformation; (2) gain a perspective of the issues, habits and needs of younger blacks; (3) gain a better grasp of the needs and concerns of black families; and (4) understand how blacks viewed their relationship with other groups.

Findings and Presentation

The findings are divided into seven sections: (1) a discussion of the characteristics of the respondents; (2) an identification of the major problems identified by the respondents; (3) attitudes about the demographic transformation; (4) attitudes and perceptions of the cultural changes; (5) views of contemporary political transformations and proposals; and (6) personal and family behavior and planning.

The discussion is complemented with findings from other national surveys, the census, and related studies and reports. The data is reported by the total percent and where relevant by age, gender, income and education. Because of the limited sample size, the subdivisions are reported with caution.

Characteristics of the Respondents

The random sample mirrored many of the demographic and institutional characteristics of the black population. The major limitation was acquiring a larger sample of blacks 35 years of age and under.

- Fifty-five percent were female and 45 percent were male.
- Thirty-eight percent were under 35 years of age.
- Fifty-four percent worked in the private sector and 25 percent in government. Ten percent were self-employed.
- Thirty-six percent were married, 33 percent were single and never married, 13 percent were divorced. Four percent were separated, 8 percent widowed, and 4 percent were unmarried but living with a partner.
- Fifty-four percent resided in the South, 19 percent in the Northeast, 19 percent in the Midwest, and 8 percent in the West.
- Among those that reported personal incomes, half made $30,000 or less and 37 percent had incomes above that level. (Twelve percent of the respondents did not provide sufficient information).
- Nearly half of the respondents were Baptist (48 percent), and 42 percent belonged to other Protestant

denominations. Five percent were Catholics, and ten percent refused to provide a religious choice or said that they did not belong to any of the major faiths.

The Most Important Problems Identified by Blacks

The five most important problems facing blacks, according to the respondents, were: racism/racial discrimination (21 percent), employment/unemployment (21 percent), education (11 percent), unity (7 percent), and crime (6 percent). Drugs (4 percent) and police brutality (4 percent) were included with crime in the analysis. The five leading problems accounted for two-thirds of the respondents' answers (Table 1). Nineteen percent identified "other" areas of concern, which were too diverse to be categorized. These problems are: apathy and self-destructiveness, "kids not being raised well," out-of-wedlock babies, and lack of spirituality and morality.

A ranking of the problems by age cohorts revealed only minor alterations. The five leading problems identified by the respondents 18-24 were unemployment, racism, education, crime, and police. This age group reported the largest number of "other" problems that were not listed on the interview guide. Among the 25-34 cohort, racism was the most frequently cited problem, followed by education, unemployment, crime and unity. This group also listed a large number of "other" problems. Racism and unemployment accounted for nearly half of the problems identified by the respondents 35 and older.

There was a close symmetry between the way blacks view their life chances and the major problems that they said faced the black community. The greatest personal concern of the respondents was unemployment/economic development (21 percent), discrimination/racism (9 percent), cost of living (9 percent), health (8 percent), and education (4 percent). These specific problems accounted for half of the total responses; 11 percent identified a broad array of "other" problems that they said would affect them in the future.

Nearly one quarter (24 percent) of the blacks 35 and under said that unemployment/economic development was the problem that they were most likely to face in the future, followed by racism (9 percent) and health (9 percent). Twenty-three percent (23 percent) cited "other" problems. Unemployment was also the leading personal concern of blacks 35-64, followed by racism. As Table 2 reveals, unemployment and racism only diminish as the leading worries after blacks reach retirement age.

Racism/Racial Discrimination

Perceptions of racism unify blacks across job and income status. Nearly two-thirds (63 percent) of the respondents said that all blacks regardless of their job status were treated unfairly by society. Blacks that reported higher incomes and higher levels of education were more inclined to say that blacks are treated unfairly. There were few differences by age (Table 3).

Blacks feel that race relations remain tolerable, but they are not sanguine about the future. Nearly half (47 percent) of the respondents indicated that race relations were only fair and more than one-third (36 percent) characterized them as poor. Only 13 percent characterized race relations as good. There were virtually no differences by age, income or education (Table 4).

When asked whether race relations would get better or worse in the next five years, 41 percent indicated that they would stay the same, 35 percent indicated that they would get better, and 19 percent suggested that it would worsen. Younger blacks were only slightly more optimistic than the older respondents. Forty-percent of the respondents 18-24 thought that relations between the races would get better, compared to 34 percent of those 55 and older. Lower-income groups were most positive than upper-income respondents. Slightly more than one-third (34 percent) of the respondents reporting incomes of $10,000 to $20,000 thought that race relations would improve, compared to 27 percent of those with incomes of $50,000 or more (Table 5).

Blacks perceive less discrimination in mortgage lending, but apprehensions about racial discrimination constrain where they look for housing. Only 19 percent of the blacks reported that they had personally been prevented from moving to a home, even if they could afford it, because of their race. Of those respondents who had tried to get a mortgage, 42 percent said that they did not experience any racial discrimination (Table 6). These findings are confirmed by other studies (Glaeser, 2001).

There are two caveats to these findings. First, nearly one-third (32 percent), of the respondents indicated that they chose not to look at certain homes because they feared they would be rejected. More than half (52 percent) of the blacks with incomes of $50,000 said that fear of rejection limited their search for homes in certain areas. Second, while blacks are obtaining more mortgages, many of them are victims of predatory lenders—sub prime lenders—who charge exorbitant interest rates (DHUD).

A major reason that racism is felt so deeply by some blacks is that it penetrates their daily activities. Twenty-seven percent (27 percent) of the respondents said that they were treated unfairly while shopping, including 28 percent of the males and an equal percentage of the females. Age does not reduce the perceptions of unfair treatment. One-third (33 percent) of the respondents 18-34 indicated that they had been treated unfairly as did 35 percent of those 45-54. Income status also failed to shield blacks against unfair treatment. An equal percentage (27 percent) of the respondents earning $10,000 to $20,000 and $50,000 and above reported that they were treated unfairly during shopping excursions (Table 7).

Blacks frequenting restaurants, bars, and other places of entertainment also reported biased treatment. Twenty-two (22 percent) of the respondents said that they were treated unfairly in these places, with one quarter (25 percent) of the males reporting mistreatment and 19 percent of the women. There were few variations by age or income. Twenty-nine percent of the blacks 18-24 reported being treated unfairly, as did one-fourth of those 45-54. Nearly three out of ten blacks earning $50,000 or more said that they were mistreated in places of entertainment (Table 8).

The League findings about black attitudes toward race relations mirror those reported in The Gallup Poll Social Audit Series. In the Gallup surveys, blacks reported pervasive mistreatment while shopping, notably in shopping malls. The Gallup polls also documented a growing pessimism among blacks. According to the Gallup surveys blacks are less likely than in earlier years to say that they are treated in the same way as whites, and 59 percent said that, "race relations will always be a problem." Like the League survey, blacks with the highest levels of education and the highest incomes often expressed the most dismal views (The Gallup Social Audit Series, February 28, 2000).

Employment/Unemployment: Black's Problematic Status in the Economic Transformation

Perceptions and charges of employment discrimination remain widespread among blacks. During the 1990s blacks filed a number of high profile discrimination suits against large corporations, including some that were noted for their exemplary "diversity" programs. Blacks have also leveled major complaints of racial discrimination against agencies within the federal government. Indeed, the head of Blacks in Government (BIG) claimed that if federal employees were financially able to bear the cost of litigation there would be a "tidal wave" of Title VI lawsuits in federal court (U.S. Commission on Civil Rights, 2001). Data from the Equal Employment Opportunity Commission (EEOC) reflect the trends in the private and public sectors. Between 1992 and 2000, blacks averaged over 28,000 complaints a year, significantly higher than complaints filed by persons of national origin, and slightly higher than those by women, who include individuals of all races (EEOC, 2001).

The League survey reflects blacks concern about racial bias in the workplace. Seventy percent (70 percent) of the respondent's indicated that they thought that blacks were discriminated against in being paid equal wages, nearly three-fourths (74 percent) said that discrimination played a role in limiting black's mobility to middle-income positions, and 79 percent said that racial discrimination played a role in promotions to higher level executive positions. Blacks over 25 years of age were more likely to attribute racial discrimination to problems of wages and mobility, suggesting that as blacks enter the workplace their perceptions of racial discrimination are heightened. The perceptions of racial discrimination also increased with an increase in income. For example, 82 percent of the respondents that reported incomes of $50,000 or more said that blacks were discriminated in being paid equal wages compared to 72 percent of those with incomes of $10,000 to $20,000 (Tables 9a – 9c).

The Gallup Organization reported similar findings. In their survey, nearly six of every ten blacks (57 percent) said that even if blacks had the same qualifications as whites they did not have a chance for getting the same job. Nearly half (47 percent) reported that they were treated less fairly than whites on the job. The polling firm suggested that the findings might be considered a "wake-up call for employers" (The Gallup Organization, February 28, 2000).

Support for affirmative action is nearly universal among blacks. Nearly four in every ten blacks reported that affirmative action had been very important in their educational and employment experiences, a proportion that increased with income and age (Table 10). And, because of the pervasive perception of racial discrimination in employment, nearly 9 of every 10 blacks in the survey (87 percent) said that there was still a need for affirmative action in higher education and places of employment. There were few differences by age cohorts, income, or education (Table 11). These findings mirror those of virtually every national survey.

Explanations for why blacks have lower incomes than whites vary by age and income. When asked to assess why the incomes of blacks were lower than whites, a little more than fifty percent (53 percent) of the respondents said that a major reason was because blacks do not have the opportunity to obtain a good education, 40 percent indicated that it was because whites are prejudiced against blacks, and 40 percent said that it resulted from a lack of motivation or willpower of blacks to pull themselves out of poverty.

Blacks with lower income and educational levels and those under 35 were more likely to cite education and lack of motivation as reasons for the lower incomes than college educated respondents with higher incomes (Table12a –12c). These responses are similar to a 1995 NBC poll, in which 32 percent of the blacks said that lack of motivation was the major reason that blacks had lower incomes than whites. The League survey findings also complement a *Newsweek* Poll, conducted by Princeton Survey Research Associates, in which nearly half (49 percent) of the blacks surveyed thought that blacks would never close the income gap with whites (*Newsweek* Poll, April 16-19, 1999).

Unemployment continues to be a major worry of blacks. Twenty-two percent of the respondents indicated that they had been unemployed in the past year, including one-third of those 18-24. As noted previously, fear of unemployment is the major personal concern of blacks. Twenty-one (21 percent) percent of the respondents reported that future unemployment was their greatest concern, a proportion that increased to 24 percent among the respondents 18-34, and 26 percent among those 25-44.

Changes in the welfare laws are forcing blacks to seek new sources of income. Sixteen percent (16 percent) of the respondents said that someone in their family had received some form of welfare in the last five years, and 14 percent of the women said that they had received assistance during that period. The 18-24 cohort had the highest proportion on welfare (16 percent) and those 55 and over the lowest (4 percent). Over one-fourth (26 percent) of the respondents with incomes under $10,000 received some form of public assistance in the past five years and 22 percent of the respondents in this income group said that someone in their family had been helped through the program. Lower-income families were not the only ones who had members on welfare. More than 10 percent of each of the income groups reported that someone in their family had been on public assistance in the last half decade (Table 13).

The personal and income options for black women with limited incomes have been significantly influenced by changes in the welfare system. The Personal Responsibility and Work Opportunity Reconciliation Act of 1996 created Temporary Assistance for Needy Families (TANF), replacing Aid to Families with Dependent Children (AFDC) and removing the major income floor for poor women. It eliminated the entitlement to welfare benefits, mandated work in exchange for public assistance, and limited the receipt of welfare to five years. Nationally, between 1996-1999, the TANF/Public Assistance rolls were cut in half, from over 12 million to 6 million persons (Department of Health and Human Services). In this survey, sixty-two percent (62 percent) of the women reported that they were able to get off welfare and find a job. However, few of them earned good wages. Nearly seventy-percent (69 percent) reported that they had incomes of $20,000 or less. (A full-time worker needs to earn $17,129 a year to be above the 1999 poverty level for a family of four) (Table 14).

Education and Schooling

Blacks' views of the public schools are in transition. The respondents presented a mixed message about the public schools. One-third indicated that they had little confidence in the ability of public schools to educate black children well and an equal proportion had some confidence. Slightly more than one-fourth (26 percent) said that they had a great deal of confidence in the public schools. While the younger cohorts had more confidence than the older age groups, there were not dramatic differences in their views. Twenty-nine (29 percent) of the 18-24 and 26 percent of the 25-34 year olds expressed great confidence in the schools compared to 21 percent of those 35-44. (Table 15).

The diversity of views was also reflected in the respondents' answers about the short-term changes in the public schools in their communities. Nearly four in ten (37 percent) said that the quality of public schools in their community would get better, one third thought they would stay the same, and one-quarter indicated that the conditions would worsen. There were virtually no differences in the age cohorts.

Blacks continue to believe that teachers have lower expectations for black students. A plurality (51 percent) of the respondents indicated that public school teachers had a lower expectation for black student performance than white students. Thirty percent (30 percent) indicated teacher expectations were the same.

Respondents reporting higher incomes were more likely to say that public school teachers held black students in lower esteem than those respondents with lower-incomes. Nearly sixty percent (57 percent) of the blacks reporting incomes of $50,000 or more said that teachers had lower expectations for black students compared to 45 percent of those with incomes between $10,000 and $20,000.

Younger blacks appeared to be especially sensitive to the issue. Over half (52 percent) of the respondents 18-24 said that teachers had lower expectations for black students and 48 percent of those 25-34 (Table 16). The League survey findings are similar to other studies.

Charter schools have become a viable option for some blacks. The question of whether to establish charter schools is one of the major policy issues within the black community. Slightly more than half of the respondents (52 percent) favored the establishment of charter schools where local school boards let parents, teachers and community members run them. Younger blacks were more likely to favor this reform than the older cohorts. Six out of every ten (60 percent) of the respondents under 35, supported charter schools in contrast to 45 percent of those 45-54, and 37 percent of those 55 and over (Table 17). In 1999, blacks constituted nearly one-fourth (24 percent) of the students in charter schools. This proportion was higher than all public schools (U.S. Department of Education, 1999).

Blacks are uncertain about the use of vouchers if tax money is diverted from public schools. While blacks in the survey generally favored the creation of charter schools, they did not support the use of tax money for vouchers to pay for children to go to private or parochial schools. Nearly sixty percent (58 percent) said that tax funds should only go to public schools while 34 percent supported public funds for vouchers. Vouchers, however, are one of the few areas, where there are distinctive differences among the age cohorts. Blacks under 45 years of age were more likely to support the use of vouchers than the respondents above that cohort. Nearly forty-percent of the respondents 18-34 (including 39 percent of those 25-34) supported vouchers as did 40 percent of the respondents 35-44 years of age. This compared with only 29 percent of those 45-64 (Table 18).

These findings mirror the surveys of The National Opinion Poll conducted for the Joint Center for Political and Economic Studies. While volatile, black's support for vouchers increased between 1997 and 1999, with those under 35 giving the greatest support to the concept (Joint Center for Political and Economic Studies, 1999).

Crime and the Police

Blacks live many paradoxes, and none more telling than their fear of crime, and their simultaneous apprehension of the police and the larger criminal justice system. Nearly twenty percent (19 percent) of the respondents reported that some member of their immediate family was currently incarcerated in a prison or juvenile detention center, a percentage that increased to 27 percent of the respondents with incomes of $10,000 to $20,000 (Table 19). Familiarity with the criminal justice system does not promote trust. Almost three-fourths of the blacks said that the criminal justice system is biased against blacks (Table 20).

But blacks also readily acknowledge their apprehension about the affect of crime and drug trafficking on their communities. Ten percent of the respondent's labeled crime and drugs a major problem facing black communities. Younger blacks were the most apprehensive: 17 percent of those aged 18-24 years old said so, as did 18 percent of those 25-34 years old. Concern was apparent across the entire group. In a poll conducted by Princeton Survey Research Associates, sixty-one percent (61 percent) of the black respondents said that crime in black neighborhoods was a major problem (Princeton Survey Research Associates/Newsweek, April 16-19, 1999).

Police/community relations remain difficult. The problematic relations between blacks and local police were a concern of all age groups. Forty-five percent of the blacks, including over half (52 percent) of the male respondents and 40 percent of the females, said that being a victim of police brutality was something that they personally worried about. Younger blacks, especially those 18-34 expressed the greatest fear. Fifty-two (52 percent) of those 18-24 said that they worried about police brutality and 56 percent of those 25-34. (Table 21). There were few differences by reported income status.

Police practices of "stop and search" are a major concern in many black communities. In this survey, forty-three percent (43 percent) of the respondents, including 62 percent of the males, indicated that the police had stopped them because of their race. This percentage was nearly identical to a 1999 Gallup poll in which 42 percent of the blacks said that they were stopped by the police because of their race.

More than half of the blacks between 25-34 reported being stopped because of their race (54 percent) and nearly half (49 percent) of all the 18-24 cohort (Table 22). It is interesting to note, that a slightly higher proportion of blacks in the upper income groups reported being stopped for racial reasons by the police. Fifty-two percent (52 percent) of the respondents reporting incomes of $50,000 or more indicated that they had been stopped compared to

49 percent of the respondents earning $10,000 to $20,000.

Slightly more than one-third of the respondents reported that the police had used more force than necessary to get them to cooperate. There were few differences by gender (36 percent of the males and 33 percent of the females) and little variation by age groups. However, lower-income respondents indicated that officers used more force than required in their confrontations (Table 23).

Unity/Black Leadership

Blacks appear to be seeking a new unity based on leaders who carry the historical civil rights banner but can fight for economic improvements. Nearly nine of every ten respondents (87 percent) indicated that civil rights is still a relevant and meaningful concept. However, they are less interested in leaders and organizations that promote racial integration and more interested in those that can deal with economic problems. Six of ten (60 percent) respondents said that the primary focus of black organizations should be to improve economic opportunities, and only 7 percent of the respondents cited racial integration as an issue of concern.

The major differences among the age cohorts are the higher proportions of younger cohorts (18-24) that said that the black community needed leaders who could deal with economic issues and provide a stronger political presence. The differential was also reflected in the educational and income status. Blacks with lower levels of education and income—mainly the youngest cohorts— were more likely to emphasize political leadership than the better educated and higher income respondents (Table 24).

The Demographic Transformation

Blacks are only part of a burgeoning population of groups of color. One of the major changes facing the black community is their reduced share of the country's population. According to the 2000 census, blacks are now the third largest group in the country. This means, among other things that race-relations, which has been historically defined in terms of black-white confrontations, is being expanded to include Hispanics, and other groups of color.

When asked if the reduction to the third largest national group was of concern to them, 44 percent indicated that it only mattered a little, one-fourth (26 percent) said that it mattered a great deal, and 20 percent said they were somewhat concerned. The age of the respondents shaped their responses. Only 21 percent of the blacks 18-34 said they were greatly concerned about the shifts, compared to 42 percent of the respondents 45 and older (Table 25).

The Cultural Transformation

Cultural changes are introducing new ideas and tensions in black civil society while reinforcing old traditions. The civil rights movement spurred a major cultural revitalization within black civil society. In a burst of introspection and critique, "Negro" became a term of derision, replaced by "black is beautiful," black or African-American designations, and a new pride in black institutions. The wave of identity and pride also sowed the seeds for a greater search among some blacks for their cross-racial-cultural roots.

Central to the cultural changes are how blacks define themselves. Nearly 8 out of every 10 respondents (78 percent) said they were "just" African American and nothing else. Nineteen percent said they were something else other than African American (The highest proportion choosing this response resided in the West). More than eighty percent (82 percent) of the blacks 18-34 said that they preferred the African-American designation, as did 74 percent of the respondents 45 and older (Table 26) .

When asked whether multi-race identification would increase or decrease African-American political power, slightly more than 4 of every 10 (41 percent) said it would decrease black power and 35 percent thought it would increase it. College graduates and respondents earning $30,000 or more were more likely to say that multi-race identifications would reduce blacks' power, while lower-income groups responded that it would lead to increased empowerment. Age differentials were less important (Table 27).

There were also differences in the perceptions of how multi-racial identifications might affect community and communal ties. Forty percent (40 percent) said that the multi-racial identifications would dilute blacks' sense of community. College graduates and higher-income respondents were more likely to hold this view than lower-income persons with limited education (Table 28).

Rap/Hip Hop: Problems of Role Models

Paralleling the internal discourse about racial identity is the issue of blacks' image in the media. Arguably, the most discordant of these issues, is the cultural role of "rap" and "hip-hop" music. When asked whether these artists were good role models, more than three-fourths (76 percent) of the respondents said "no" and only 13 percent responded affirmatively. The older and the better educated the respondents the more negatively they responded. However, nearly two-thirds (65 percent) of the respondents 18-24 also said that the artists were poor role models and only 25 percent said they provided positive images for youth (Table 29).

It should be noted that while "rap" artists are not viewed as positive role models, blacks have reported in other surveys that there are not enough successful blacks for young people to look up to (Princeton Survey Research Associates, April 16-19,1999).

Disparate Views of Black Images on Television

The respondents also showed disdain for the way blacks are portrayed on television. Slightly more than two-thirds (67 percent) of the respondents said that blacks were not accurately portrayed on TV shows, including 71 percent of the blacks between the ages of 18-34.

Respondents with higher levels of income and education were especially disdainful of black portrayals on television. Eighty-one percent of the respondents with a college degree found the portrayals distasteful and 76 percent of those who reported incomes of $50,000 or more. By contrast 46 percent of the respondents with less than a high school education said that the portrayals were accurate as did 40 percent of those who earned $10,000 or less (Table 30).

The League survey complements and expands other findings. In other surveys, blacks have indicated that there are too few black actors and actresses on prime time TV shows (Gallup Poll, November 16,1999). The League survey suggests that it is not merely the number of actors but the quality and type of their portrayals.

The discussion of the media, and television in particular, deserves more attention. Although, blacks do not like their portrayals on television, they watch on average more hours of television than any other group (Neilsen Report *www.neilsenmedia.com/eth-nicmeasure/african-american/AA primetime.html*). A plurality (54 percent) of the respondents reported that they got most of their news information from television, and one quarter relied on mainstream newspapers. Only one percent said they read black newspapers as a principal source of news. Television is especially important to women and lower-income groups. Nearly sixty-percent (58 percent) of the women in the survey said that television served as their principal news source compared to 48 percent of the men. Sixty-two percent of the respondents with incomes of $10,000 to $20,000 relied on television for news, compared to 46 percent of those with incomes over $50,000 (Table 31).

Reading Books

Books are a source of cultural maintenance and educational growth. Nearly one third (31 percent) of the blacks in the survey said that they did not read any books (14 percent) or read one to four a year (27 percent). Among the 18-24 cohort, 11 percent reported that they did not read any books, 11 percent said they read 25 or more, and 32 percent said that they read one to four a year. In the 25-34 age group, 28 percent reported reading 10-24 books a year and 18 percent read twenty-five or more.

Nearly half (46 percent) of the respondents with incomes between $10,000 and $20,000 reported that they either read no books or read less than five a year, compared to 32 percent of those with incomes of $50,000 or more (Table 32).

The resilience of the black church as a cultural and political institution. Like most Americans, blacks say that religion is important in their lives. More than three-fourths (78 percent) of the respondents reported that religion was extremely important and 15 percent indicated that it was fairly important. Among Baptists, the major black denomination, 85 percent reported that religion was extremely important.

The importance of religion increased with age. However, younger blacks also said that religion played an important role in their lives. In the 18-24 cohort, nearly sixty percent (59 percent) said that religion was extremely important and 31 percent reported that it was fairly important. Nearly eighty percent (79 percent) of the blacks 25-34 claimed that religion was extremely important and more than 80 percent of the cohorts 35 and older.

Overall, 25 percent of the respondents said that they attended religious services more than once a week. Among respondents who reported that religion was very important the percentage climbed to 95 percent (Table 33).

Political Transformations: Tensions of Old Party Allegiances and New Proposals

While blacks continue to support the Democratic Party, they increasingly embrace more "conservative" proposals. Nearly two-thirds (64 percent) of the blacks in the survey said that politicians and the political system could not be trusted to "do the right thing." However, when asked which of the political parties was most committed to dealing with black problems, they overwhelmingly chose the Democratic Party.

Three fourths of the respondents identified themselves as Democrats, and six of every ten said that the Democratic Party is committed to the issues most important to blacks. Only 10 percent of the blacks said that the Republican Party had a commitment to dealing with their problems, and nearly half (49 percent) disapproved of the job that George Bush was doing as President.

Age, gender, education and income are useful benchmarks of political attitudes. Black women were slightly more likely to say that the Democratic Party was committed to black issues than men (62 to 58 percent). Older blacks were more committed to the Democratic Party than younger cohorts, as were respondents with less than a high school education and lower incomes. (Tables 34a and 34b).

These findings are similar to those reported by the Joint Center of Political and Economic Studies from the National Opinion Polls. In their survey an almost equal proportion to that of the League (74 percent) identified themselves as Democrats. Blacks also said that they supported the Democratic Party because they believed it would deal with issues of concern to them. Many of those issues were identified in the League survey, notably race relations, and unemployment (Joint Center for Political and Economic Studies, 2000).

Despite the commitment to the Democratic Party, blacks have

embraced some of the proposals associated with Republicans and conservatives. Support for the faith-based initiative program proposed by President Bush was especially strong. Exactly 50 percent favored the proposal, which would allow religious groups to administer government programs to the needy, compared to 32 percent against it. That high level of support is consistent with Americans' view that local churches are influential community resources. Nearly one third (32 percent) of the respondents said that local churches were the most influential organizations in their community, a proportion that increases for women (36 percent) and persons who reported incomes of $10,000 to $20,000 (37 percent). Younger blacks, notably those 18-24, were more likely to say that churches were only one of several influential community organizations (Table 35).

Blacks' support for faith-based organizations is consistent with national trends. A survey by the Pew Partnership for Civic Change found that 56 percent of Americans looked to faith based institutions to solve social problems, a percentage second only to the local police departments (The Pew Partnership for Civic Change).

Individual business ownership is gaining support among blacks. Although the pace of new black businesses is lower than Hispanics and Asians, there has been a steady rise in ownership in recent decades (Survey of Minority Owned Business Enterprises, 1997; Office of Advocacy, U.S. Small Business Administration, 1999). In this survey only 10 percent of the respondents worked for themselves but more than two-thirds (67 percent) said that they wanted to own their own business in the future. Business ownership had a greater appeal to males (71 percent) than women (63 percent). It also holds great appeal to younger blacks. Nearly 8 of every 10 blacks 18-34 said they wanted to own their own business and 83 percent of those 25-34. (Table 36).

Black Families: Planning for the Future

Many blacks view the family as the most important organization for improving the situation of black families. The status of black families remains a critical concern among the respondents. Nearly half (47 percent) of the respondents said that individual and family initiatives were the best way to improve the situation of black families.

Churches were viewed as the second most important source of assistance to black families, and community organizations ranked third.

Blacks under 45 years of age, college graduates, and respondents with incomes of $30,000 or more were much more sanguine about the ability of individuals and families to improve the status of black families than those in their later years or persons with limited education. Among respondents with less than a high school education, the church was the most important unit for helping black families (Table 37).

Blacks have limited resources to secure themselves and their families for the long term. Only about 4 in 10 blacks (42 percent) are enrolled in pension plans other than social security. The proportion of younger blacks, 35-44 with other plans, was higher than those 65 and above (54 to 40 percent). Less than 40 percent of the respondents with incomes under $30,000 had stocks or mutual funds (Table 38).

Although stocks and mutual funds are recognized as important assets for long-term security, blacks are poorly invested in both. According to the Federal Reserve Board and the Securities Industry Association, more than half of all Americans own stocks (The Federal Reserve data for 1998 showed that 49 percent of all Americans have direct or indirect-mutual funds-stock holdings http://www.federalreserve.gov). However in this survey, only 36 percent of the respondents belonged to a mutual fund or were invested in stocks.

Income was a major deterrent. Less than 40 percent of the respondents earning $30,000 or less were invested in the market, compared to 79 percent of those with incomes of $50,000 or more. Less than half of each of the age cohorts was invested in mutual funds and stocks, including only 17 percent of the respondents 65 and older (For a similar story, see Farzad, Smart Money, February 8, 2001).

The respondents, notably the lower-income blacks carried substantial debt. Nearly one-third of the blacks said that, excluding a mortgage; they owed more than $5,000 to creditors (Table 39).

Despite their limited resources, Blacks expect to improve their standard of living in the future. Nearly three-fourths (72 percent) of the respondents reported that they expected to have greater financial security than their parents. The optimism is greatest among the younger cohorts. Three-fourths of the 18-24 year olds said that their financial status would be better compared to 62 percent of the respondents in the 45-54 age group (Table 40). There was almost universal accord among the respondents that they and their families had a good chance of improving their standard of living. Nearly nine of every ten (86 percent) agreed with the statement that "people like me have a good chance of improving their standard of living."

A higher proportion of black males than females expect to get married. Although only slightly more than one third (36 percent) of the respondents were married, nearly sixty percent (57 percent) of the unmarried respondents expected to get married in the future. The expectations were highest among the 18-34 cohort, 61 percent of whom had never been married.

The proportion of males who expected to get married was much higher than women. While 68 percent of the males said they expect get married in the future only 49 percent of the females were hopeful of such a union. Blacks with lower incomes and education were also less likely to look forward to marriage (Table 41).

If they get married in the future, 71 percent of the respondents indicated that they would like to marry someone with equal or more education. Women were slightly more interested in mates with more education than men (36 to 33 percent).

Contracting HIV is a Concern, but Not a Major One

HIV/AIDS is a major problem among Blacks. It is estimated that in 1998, 240,000-325,000 blacks—about 1 in 50 men and 1 in 160 women—were infected with HIV, and almost 118,000 were living with AIDS (Center for Communicable Diseases, 2000). It's pervasiveness in the black community spurred black political and civic leaders to intensify their own efforts to address the problems. In June, about 80 office holders, health experts and religious leaders met in Atlanta to develop what they said would be a disease-fighting agenda. They said they would present their document to President Bush.

Despite warnings from CBC and public and private agencies,

nearly three-fourths (72 percent) of the respondents indicated that they were not too worried about contracting HIV.

Younger cohorts, notably those 18-24 expressed the greatest worry about contracting the virus. However, the proportion was small. Only one fourth (24 percent) of the 18-24 year olds said that they were very worried, while 55 percent indicated that they were not too concerned. There were few differences by gender. However, lower-income respondents indicated a much greater concern than those with higher incomes. Twenty-four percent of the group earning $10,000 to 20,000 said that they were very worried about contracting HIV compared to 6 percent of those earning $50,000 or more (Table 42).

The respondents were almost evenly divided on whether they had made any behavioral changes because of their concern about HIV. About half of the respondents (48 percent) reported that they had changed their behavior to avoid contracting HIV and half (49 percent) said they had not made any changes in their behavior. Younger blacks reported the greatest changes. Among the 18-24 year olds, 63 percent reported that they had changed their personal behavior and 57 percent of the 25-34 cohort. A higher proportion of males (53 percent) said that they changed their behavior than female (44 percent).

Conclusion

Transformations, whatever their origin, inevitably require modifications in the institutional as well as individual policies and behavior. Transformations also expose—sometimes brutally—racial and economic inequalities: magnifying gaps that seemed to be closing, and posing new questions about policies and programs that once appeared sacrosanct. A half-century ago, few people understood the potential power of the computer; few predicted the near decimation of the New Deal welfare program, and few forecast the demographic transformation, in which groups of color would alter the historical proportions among the races.

Blacks have been no different than other groups in their inability to forecast the transformations. However, this survey suggests that the transformations are often accentuating the racial divide between whites and blacks, particularly among lower-income blacks. Racial discrimination also continues to shadow the life chances of African Americans at all levels, including, despite rhetoric to the contrary, younger blacks, proving again, that despite the best efforts of generations of black parents and black institutions to shield their youth from racial bias, it still menaces their maturation. Indeed, the pervasive sense of racial discrimination among the more prosperous blacks in this survey is a signal reminder that neither age nor income provides an escape from the capriciousness of individual prejudice or the systemic weight of institutional racism.

A major question facing Black America, of course, is how black leadership will respond to and attempt to influence these transformations. One of the clearest outcomes of the contemporary changes are the broadening array of policy options being discussed in legislative arenas for dealing with income and other structural inequalities. Increasingly, few of these options reflect the conventional civil rights approaches to issues of inequality. The growing if uncertain black support for charter schools, vouchers, and faith-based initiatives—particularly among younger blacks—is the clearest manifestation of these internal changes. Younger blacks now say that while they believe in civil rights, they want leaders who can deal with employment and economic development. They, like older blacks support the black church as a leading cultural and political force, but they also place more value on a variety of community institutions.

The power of the black experience—embedded in black civic and religious institutions—has been the historical determination of its participants not to allow racism to become fully debilitating. Perhaps the greatest struggle during the transformations is how to keep these institutions relevant while reviving them for the task ahead.

Footnotes

[1]Hispanic may be of any race. By 2050, they are projected to be 24 percent of the population, and blacks will constitute 13 percent.

References

The Gallup Organization, Princeton, "Perceptions of Black and White Americans Continue to Diverge Widely on Issues of Race Relations in the U.S." February 28, 2000.

Glaeser, Edward. Racial Segregation in the 2000 Census: Promising News, Center on Urban and Metropolitan Policy, April 2001, The Brookings Institution.

The Equal Employment Opportunity Commission, Race-Based Charges FY 1992-2000, Office of Research, Information, and Planning, Washington, 2001.

Bositis, David, National Opinion Poll: Education 1999, Washington D.C.

Bositis, David, National Opinion Poll: Politics 2000, Washington D.C.

Frey, William, Census 2000 Shows Large Black Return to the South, Reinforcing the Region's "White-Black" Demographic Profile, (Ann Arbor: Population Studies Center, May 2001).

U.S. Census Bureau. 1997. Economic Census, Survey of Minority-Owned Business Enterprises Washington D.C.

U.S. Department of Commerce. October 2000. Falling Through the Net: Toward Digital Inclusion.

The Pew Partnership for Civic Change. 2001. "Nonprofit, faith-based groups near the top of poll on solving social problems." *Washington Post*, February 1, 2000.

Wolff, Edward. 1983-1998. Recent Trends in Wealth Ownership.

Raines, Franklin. Faith-Based Charity Works, *Wall Street Journal*, Feb 15, 2001.

U.S. Civil Rights Commission. 2001. A Bridge to One America: The Civil Rights Performance of the Clinton Administration Washington, D.C.

Table 1. Five Most Important Problems Facing Blacks Today

All ages		Ages 18-24		Ages 25-34	
Racism	21.3%	Unemployment	19.1%	Racism	18.5%
Unemployment	20.7%	Racism	13.9%	Education	17.8%
Education	11.2%	Education	10.4%	Unemployment	17.5%
Unity	6.9%	Crime	9.4%	Crime	7.9%
Crime	6.1%	Police	5.7%	Unity	7.1%
Total	66.2%				

Ages 35-44		Ages 45-54		Ages 55 and above	
Racism	24.6%	Racism	24.9%	Racism	24.0%
Unemployment	23.8%	Unemployment	22.8%	Unemployment	21.4%
Unity	8.9%	Education	10.7%	Education	8.3%
Education	8.5%	Unity	8.8%	Unity	6.0%
Crime	5.3%	Drugs	4.2%	Job Training	4.7%

Table 2. Five Most Important Personal Problems Blacks Will Face in the Next 10 Years

All ages		Ages 18-24		Ages 24-34	
Unemployment	21.1%	Unemployment	19.1%	Racism	18.5%
Racism	9.3%	Racism	13.9%	Education	17.8%
Cost of Living	9.2%	Education	10.4%	Unemployment	17.5%
Health	7.5%	Crime	9.4%	Crime	7.9%
Education	4.2%	Police	5.7%	Unity	7.1%
Total	51.3%				

Ages 35-44		Ages 45-54		Ages 55 and above	
Racism	24.6%	Racism	24.9%	Racism	24.0%
Unemployment	23.8%	Unemployment	22.8%	Unemployment	21.4%
Unity	8.9%	Education	10.7%	Education	8.3%
Education	8.5%	Unity	8.8%	Unity	6.0%
Crime	5.3%	Drugs	4.2%	Job Training	4.7%

Table 3. Are only low-income African Americans treated unfairly by society or are all African Americans, even including those with good jobs, treated unfairly?

Age Group	Only Low Income are Treated Unfairly	All Blacks are Treated Unfairly	All Blacks are Treated Fairly
18–24	23.8%	62.2%	9.1%
25–34	23.8%	63.8%	6.3%
35–44	17.2%	63.3%	8.3%
45–54	20.5%	65.4%	5.5%
55 and above	22.0%	61.0%	6.0%
Total	21.2%	63.0%	7.1%
By Income			
<$10,000	26.2%	53.3%	12.3%
$10–20,000	30.9%	59.2%	2.6%
$20–30,000	12.0%	69.6%	9.6%
$30–50,000	21.6%	67.4%	4.2%
$50,000 +	14.4%	73.7%	5.9%
Total	21.5%	64.6%	6.5%

Table 4. The State of Race Relations in America Today

Age Group	Excellent	Good	Only Fair	Poor
18–24	2.1%	17.4%	45.8%	31.9%
25–34	0.0%	11.3%	52.8%	31.4%
35–44	1.1%	9.5%	46.9%	40.8%
45–54	1.6%	12.6%	48.8%	34.6%
55 and above	1.1%	13.3%	47.3%	35.6%
Total	1.1%	13.3%	47.3%	35.6%
By Income				
<$10,000	0.0%	22.1%	41.8%	29.5%
$10–20,000	0.0%	13.1%	49.7%	35.5%
$20–30,000	0.8%	8.7%	54.3%	34.6%
$30–50,000	1.1%	11.6%	46.3%	40.0%
$50,000 +	0.8%	13.6%	50.0%	34.7%
Total	0.6%	13.5%	48.3%	35.4%

Table 5. The State of Race Relations During the Next Five Years

Age Group	Better	Worse	Stay the Same
18–24	39.9%	18.9%	38.5%
25–34	34.0%	17.6%	43.4%
35–44	30.2%	25.7%	39.7%
45–54	35.4%	17.3%	40.9%
55 and above	34.3%	16.6%	42.0%
Total	34.6%	19.4%	40.5%
By Income			
<$10,000	35.8%	16.3%	42.3%
$10–20,000	33.3%	22.2%	37.9%
$20–30,000	34.9%	18.3%	42.1%
$30–50,000	35.4%	21.7%	40.2%
$50,000 +	27.4%	22.2%	46.2%
Total	33.6%	20.3%	41.4%

Table 6. Have you personally experienced racial discrimination when applying for a mortgage?

Age Group	Experienced Discrimination	Has not Experienced Discrimination	Never Applied for Mortgage
18–24	7.7%	16.8%	74.8%
25–34	10.7%	35.2%	53.5%
35–44	15.5%	51.4%	32.6%
45–54	17.2%	50.0%	28.9%
55 and above	18.1%	51.6%	27.5%
Total	13.8%	41.8%	42.5%
By Income			
<$10,000	9.9%	28.9%	59.5%
$10–20,000	11.8%	29.6%	58.6%
$20–30,000	9.6%	42.4%	48.0%
$30–50,000	16.4%	52.4%	28.6%
$50,000 +	21.8%	59.7%	16.8%
Total	14.0%	42.9%	41.8%

45

Table 7. Were you treated unfairly in a store in the last 30 days?

Age Group	Yes	No	By Income	Yes	No
18–24	32.6%	67.4%	<$10,000	23.0%	75.9%
25–34	34.4%	62.5%	$10–20,000	26.8%	73.2%
35–44	27.8%	71.1%	$20–30,000	29.4%	69.8%
45–54	34.6%	63.8%	$30–50,000	31.2%	68.3%
55 and above	11.0%	86.3%	$50,000 +	27.1%	71.2%
Total	27.1%	71.1%	Total	27.8%	71.3%

Table 8. Were you treated unfairly in a place of entertainment in the last 30 days?

Age Group	Yes	No	By Income	Yes	No
18–24	29.2%	70.8%	<$10,000	19.7%	78.7%
25–34	29.6%	68.6%	$10–20,000	20.9%	78.4%
35–44	21.7%	77.8%	$20–30,000	21.4%	77.0%
45–54	25.0%	71.9%	$30–50,000	22.1%	77.9%
55 and above	7.7%	89.6%	$50,000 +	27.1%	72.0%
Total	21.8%	76.4%	Total	22.1%	77.0%

Table 9a. Are blacks discriminated against in being paid equal wages?

Age Group	Yes	No	By Income	Yes	No
18–24	58.0%	35.0%	<$10,000	57.4%	32.0%
25–34	70.4%	23.3%	$10–20,000	71.9%	22.2%
35–44	72.2%	21.7%	$20–30,000	66.7%	26.2%
45–54	73.4%	18.0%	$30–50,000	76.8%	17.4%
55 and above	74.0%	16.6%	$50,000 +	82.2%	16.1%
Total	70.0%	22.5%	Total	71.5%	22.3%

Table 9b. Are blacks discriminated against in being promoted to middle-level positions? Management positions?

Age Group	Yes	No	By Income	Yes	No
18-24	60.4%	34.7%	<$10,000	59.8%	30.3%
25-34	71.1%	23.3%	$10-20,000	77.8%	16.3%
35-44	81.1%	12.8%	$20-30,000	77.0%	15.9%
45-54	81.1%	15.0%	$30-50,000	78.8%	20.1%
55 and above	77.5%	15.4%	$50,000 +	84.7%	14.4%
Total	74.4%	19.7%	Total	76.0%	19.4%

Table 9c. Are blacks discriminated against in being promoted to high level executive positions?

Age Group	Yes	No	By Income	Yes	No
18-24	67.1%	29.4%	<$10,000	62.8%	26.4%
25-34	79.2%	15.1%	$10-20,000	81.0%	15.7%
35-44	82.2%	13.3%	$20-30,000	83.5%	11.8%
45-54	83.5%	12.6%	$30-50,000	87.9%	11.6%
55 and above	83.0%	11.0%	$50,000 +	89.0%	9.3%
Total	79.3%	15.9%	Total	81.5%	14.7%

Table 10. How important a role did affirmative action play in your own educational or employment experience?

Age Group	Very Important	Somewhat Important	Not Important
18-24	30.6%	37.5%	30.6%
25-34	41.5%	26.4%	30.2%
35-44	41.1%	28.3%	28.3%
45-54	42.2%	25.8%	27.3%
55 and above	40.1%	29.1%	26.9%
Total	39.3%	29.3%	28.4%
By Income			
<$10,000	48.4%	32.8%	14.8%
$10-20,000	36.8%	32.9%	28.3%
$20-30,000	35.4%	27.6%	36.2%
$30-50,000	40.0%	26.3%	30.5%
$50,000 +	40.7%	27.1%	32.2%
Total	40.1%	29.2%	28.6%

Table 11. Is affirmative action still needed in higher education and places of employment?

Age Group	Yes	No	By Income	Yes	No
18–24	81.3%	15.3%	<$10,000	86.9%	7.4%
25–34	87.4%	6.9%	$10–20,000	88.2%	7.2%
35–44	92.2%	6.1%	$20–30,000	89.7%	9.5%
45–54	85.9%	9.4%	$30–50,000	89.9%	9.0%
55 and above	88.5%	4.9%	$50,000 +	86.4%	11.9%
Total	87.0%	8.2%	Total	88.1%	8.9%

Table 12a. Do blacks have lower incomes than whites because blacks don't have the chance for a good education?

Age Group	Major Reason	Minor Reason	Not a Reason
18–24	56.3%	25.0%	18.1%
25–34	54.7%	25.2%	18.2%
35–44	51.9%	22.7%	20.4%
45–54	51.9%	29.5%	15.5%
55 and above	50.0%	26.4%	18.1%
Total	53.0%	25.4%	18.2%
By Income			
<$10,000	51.6%	23.0%	20.5%
$10–20,000	53.6%	27.5%	16.3%
$20–30,000	54.8%	27.0%	15.9%
$30–50,000	56.8%	23.7%	17.9%
$50,000 +	51.7%	26.3%	21.2%
Total	54.0%	25.4%	18.2%

Table 12b. Do blacks have lower incomes than whites because most whites are prejudiced against blacks?

Age Group	Major Reason	Minor Reason	Not a Reason
18-24	34.3%	45.5%	20.3%
25-34	37.1%	43.4%	15.7%
35-44	38.9%	32.8%	23.3%
45-54	39.4%	42.5%	12.6%
55 and above	47.8%	29.7%	16.5%
Total	40.1%	37.9%	17.8%
By Income			
<$10,000	43.8%	29.8%	21.5%
$10-20,000	39.2%	37.3%	19.6%
$20-30,000	39.4%	40.9%	17.3%
$30-50,000	40.0%	43.2%	15.8%
$50,000 +	39.0%	42.4%	15.3%
Total	40.2%	39.1%	17.8%

Table 12c. Do blacks have lower incomes than whites because most blacks don't have the motivation and willpower to pull themselves out of poverty?

Age Group	Major Reason	Minor Reason	Not a Reason
18-24	46.5%	31.9%	21.5%
25-34	45.9%	28.3%	24.5%
35-44	36.1%	32.2%	29.4%
45-54	37.8%	25.2%	32.3%
55 and above	36.5%	22.7%	32.6%
Total	40.1%	28.0%	28.3%
By Income			
<$10,000	47.9%	23.1%	26.4%
$10-20,000	45.1%	25.5%	25.5%
$20-30,000	44.4%	30.2%	23.8%
$30-50,000	36.5%	30.2%	32.2%
$50,000 +	28.0%	36.4%	32.3%
Total	40.3%	29.0%	28.3%

Table 13. Have you been on Welfare in the past five years?

Age Group	Yes	No	By Income	Yes	No
18-24	16.1%	82.5%	<$10,000	26.2%	73.0%
25-34	12.6%	86.8%	$10-20,000	11.8%	88.2%
35-44	7.2%	92.8%	$20-30,000	7.9%	92.1%
45-54	7.9%	90.6%	$30-50,000	3.2%	96.3%
55 and above	3.9%	94.5%	$50,000 +	0.8%	99.2%
Total	9.3%	89.6%	Total	9.5%	90.3%

Table 14. If you were on welfare in the past five years were you able to get off and obtain a full-time job?

Age Group	Yes	No	By Income	Yes	No
18-24	66.7%	25.0%	<$10,000	53.1%	40.6%
25-34	65.0%	30.0%	$10-20,000	77.8%	16.7%
35-44	61.5%	38.5%	$20-30,000	100.0%	0.0%
45-54	60.0%	40.0%	$30-50,000	50.0%	50.0%
55 and above	25.0%	75.0%	$50,000 +	0.0%	100.0%
Total	59.2%	36.8%	Total	65.7%	29.9%

Table 15. Do you have confidence in the public school system?

Age Group	Great Deal of Confidence	Some Confidence	Little Confidence
18-24	29.2%	32.6%	28.5%
25-34	25.8%	37.1%	30.2%
35-44	21.0%	37.0%	37.0%
45-54	26.6%	29.7%	39.1%
55 and above	30.4%	28.2%	32.0%
Total	26.4%	33.0%	33.3%
By Income			
<$10,000	35.2%	36.1%	22.1%
$10-20,000	24.8%	30.1%	36.6%
$20-30,000	25.4%	34.9%	34.9%
$30-50,000	27.0%	31.2%	34.4%
$50,000 +	20.3%	34.7%	35.6%
Total	26.6%	33.1%	33.1%

Table 16. Do you think public school teachers have the the same level of expectations of black students as white students?

Age Group	Higher	Lower	Same
18-24	11.1%	52.1%	34.0%
25-34	10.7%	48.4%	33.3%
35-44	7.2%	56.7%	26.7%
45-54	4.7%	60.6%	27.6%
55 and above	12.7%	39.2%	31.5%
Total	9.5%	50.7%	30.3%
By Income			
<$10,000	15.6%	39.3%	36.1%
$10-20,000	11.8%	44.4%	34.6%
$20-30,000	8.7%	57.1%	26.2%
$30-50,000	6.3%	57.1%	27.5%
$50,000 +	5.1%	57.3%	29.1%
Total	9.3%	51.3%	30.6%

Table 17. Do you favor or oppose charter schools?

Age Group	Favor	Oppose	By Income	Favor	Oppose
18-24	61.5%	30.8%	<$10,000	50.0%	38.5%
25-34	58.5%	28.3%	$10-20,000	55.6%	12.4%
35-44	58.3%	27.8%	$20-30,000	56.3%	18.3%
45-54	45.3%	38.3%	$30-50,000	45.8%	14.2%
55 and above	37.0%	45.9%	$50,000 +	61.9%	9.3%
Total	51.8%	34.1%	Total	53.2%	13.3%

Table 18. Do you think some tax money should be used for vouchers to help pay for children to go to private school or parochial school or all education tax money should be used for only public schools?

Age Group	Vouchers	Only public schools	By Income	Vouchers	Only public schools
18–24	37.5%	55.6%	<$10,000	38.5%	54.9%
25–34	39.0%	53.5%	$10–20,000	35.3%	59.5%
35–44	40.3%	50.3%	$20–30,000	35.7%	54.8%
45–54	34.4%	60.2%	$30–50,000	26.8%	64.7%
55 and above	19.9%	71.3%	$50,000 +	39.8%	56.8%
Total	33.8%	58.4%	Total	34.4%	58.8%

Table 19. Is a member of the respondent's immediate family currently incarcerated in a prison or juvenile detention facility?

Age Group	Yes	No	By Income	Yes	No
18–24	22.2%	77.8%	<$10,000	24.0%	75.2%
25–34	22.0%	76.7%	$10–20,000	27.5%	71.9%
35–44	16.7%	82.2%	$20–30,000	20.6%	79.4%
45–54	23.6%	74.0%	$30–50,000	16.9%	82.5%
55 and above	15.5%	81.2%	$50,000 +	13.6%	86.4%
Total	19.4%	78.8%	Total	20.5%	79.1%

Table 20. Do you think the criminal justice system in the U.S. is biased in favor of blacks, against blacks or does it generally give blacks a fair treatment?

Age Group	Favor Blacks	Against Blacks	Fair to blacks
18-24	0.7%	69.9%	21.0%
25-34	0.6%	77.5%	13.8%
35-44	1.1%	75.6%	15.6%
45-54	0.8%	78.0%	11.8%
55 and above	1.6%	66.5%	14.3%
Total	1.0%	73.4%	15.1%
By Income			
<$10,000	0.8%	60.7%	27.0%
$10-20,000	1.3%	78.3%	9.9%
$20-30,000	0.8%	76.2%	15.1%
$30-50,000	1.1%	81.0%	12.7%
$50,000 +	0.8%	78.0%	12.7%
Total	1.0%	75.5%	15.0%

Table 21. Are you worried about being a victim of police brutality?

Age Group	Yes	No	By Income	Yes	No
18-24	51.7%	47.6%	<$10,000	41.8%	54.9%
25-34	56.0%	42.8%	$10-20,000	55.6%	44.4%
35-44	37.8%	62.2%	$20-30,000	45.2%	54.8%
45-54	51.2%	47.2%	$30-50,000	42.9%	57.1%
55 and above	34.8%	62.4%	$50,000 +	42.4%	57.6%
Total	45.2%	53.4%	Total	45.8%	53.7%

Table 22. Have you ever felt that you were stopped by the police just because of race or ethnic background?

Age Group	Yes	No	By Income	Yes	No
18-24	48.6%	48.6%	<$10,000	27.3%	69.4%
25-34	53.5%	45.3%	$10-20,000	49.0%	51.0%
35-44	43.3%	55.0%	$20-30,000	42.9%	57.1%
45-54	45.7%	52.8%	$30-50,000	46.6%	52.4%
55 and above	29.7%	69.2%	$50,000 +	52.5%	47.5%
Total	43.1%	55.1%	Total	44.1%	55.0%

Table 23. If in the last five years you have been upset about the way a police officer behaved towards you, was it because you felt the police used more force than necessary to get you to cooperate?

Age Group	Yes	No	By Income	Yes	No
18–24	43.7%	54.9%	<$10,000	47.2%	52.8%
25–34	31.4%	65.7%	$10–20,000	40.0%	58.2%
35–44	27.1%	71.2%	$20–30,000	35.6%	64.4%
45–54	36.8%	63.2%	$30–50,000	29.3%	69.3%
55 and above	34.4%	62.5%	$50,000 +	31.7%	63.4%
Total	35.1%	63.1%	Total	35.7%	62.7%

Table 24. What do you personally think should be the primary focus of black organizations?

Age Group	Economic Opportunity	Integration	Political Leadership
18–24	49.7%	7.0%	32.9%
25–34	68.6%	3.1%	19.5%
35–44	60.6%	9.4%	21.7%
45–54	64.6%	3.9%	24.4%
55 and above	54.7%	9.9%	24.3%
Total	59.6%	6.9%	24.2%
By Income			
<$10,000	53.3%	9.0%	27.9%
$10–20,000	61.4%	5.2%	27.5%
$20–30,000	59.1%	7.1%	26.0%
$30–50,000	68.3%	5.8%	19.0%
$50,000 +	64.7%	7.6%	19.3%
Total	62.0%	6.8%	23.7%

Table 25. Are you concerned about the fact that blacks will soon become the third largest group in the U.S. instead of the second largest?

Age Group	A Great Deal Concerned	Somewhat Concerned	Little Concerned
18-24	17.4%	22.2%	48.6%
25-34	23.8%	18.1%	48.1%
35-44	23.9%	22.2%	45.6%
45-54	33.9%	15.7%	38.6%
55 and above	30.8%	19.8%	36.8%
Total	25.9%	19.8%	43.5%
By Income			
<$10,000	21.5%	19.8%	46.3%
$10-20,000	24.3%	16.4%	48.7%
$20-30,000	29.4%	19.8%	46.8%
$30-50,000	27.9%	20.0%	38.9%
$50,000 +	17.8%	20.3%	50.0%
Total	24.6%	19.2%	45.5%

Table 26. When identifying your race, do you consider yourself as African American or African American and something else?

Age Group	African American	African American and Something Else
18-24	43.7%	54.9%
25-34	31.4%	65.7%
35-44	27.1%	71.2%
45-54	36.8%	63.2%
55 and above	34.4%	62.5%
Total	35.1%	63.1%
By Income		
<$10,000	47.2%	52.8%
$10-20,000	40.0%	58.2%
$20-30,000	35.6%	64.4%
$30-50,000	39.3%	69.3%
$50,000 +	31.7%	63.4%
Total	35.7%	62.7%

55

Table 27. Do you think this multi-race identification will increase or decrease African-Amerian political power?

Age Group	Increase	Decrease	By Income	Increase	Decrease
18-24	40.3%	41.0%	<$10,000	43.0%	30.6%
25-34	36.5%	41.5%	$10-20,000	40.8%	32.9%
35-44	30.0%	43.3%	$20-30,000	40.2%	38.6%
45-54	25.8%	46.9%	$30-50,000	30.2%	51.3%
55 and above	40.1%	33.0%	$50,000 +	21.2%	50.8%
Total	34.8%	40.4%	Total	34.9%	41.4%

Table 28. Do you think multi-race identification will increase or decrease African Americans' sense of community?

Age Group	Increase	Decrease	By Income	Increase	Decrease
18-24	41.7%	38.9%	<$10,000	39.8%	34.1%
25-34	36.9%	40.0%	$10-20,000	40.8%	36.8%
35-44	35.9%	39.8%	$20-30,000	37.8%	43.3%
45-54	23.8%	51.6%	$30-50,000	31.7%	46.6%
55 and above	40.3%	34.3%	$50,000 +	24.6%	44.1%
Total	36.1%	40.1%	Total	35.0%	41.3%

Table 29. Do you think hip-hop and rap artists are good role models for black children and teenagers?

Age Group	Yes	No	By Income	Yes	No
18-24	24.5%	65.0%	<$10,000	16.4%	76.2%
25-34	16.4%	71.1%	$10-20,000	15.0%	70.6%
35-44	10.6%	77.8%	$20-30,000	15.1%	76.2%
45-54	6.3%	82.8%	$30-50,000	8.9%	81.1%
55 and above	8.3%	84.5%	$50,000 +	9.2%	84.0%
Total	13.0%	76.1%	Total	12.7%	77.6%

Table 30. Do you think blacks are accurately portrayed on TV shows?

Age Group	Yes	No	By Income	Yes	No
18-24	32.6%	65.3%	<$10,000	39.7%	47.9%
25-34	18.2%	75.5%	$10-20,000	26.1%	67.3%
35-44	22.8%	64.4%	$20-30,000	21.4%	72.2%
45-54	22.0%	71.7%	$30-50,000	20.0%	73.7%
55 and above	24.9%	61.9%	$50,000 +	16.0%	75.6%
Total	24.1%	67.0%	Total	24.3%	68.0%

Table 31. From which of the sources do you get most of your news information?

Age Group	Mainstream Newspapers	Black Newspapers	Magazines	Radio	TV	Internet	Tabloids
18-24	21.7%	0.0%	1.4%	9.1%	53.8%	4.2%	0.0%
25-34	25.0%	1.9%	0.6%	10.6%	48.8%	6.9%	0.0%
35-44	27.8%	1.1%	2.8%	7.2%	51.1%	2.8%	0.0%
45-54	28.1%	1.6%	1.6%	3.1%	56.3%	3.1%	0.8%
55 and above	22.1%	2.2%	1.1%	3.9%	59.7%	1.7%	1.1%
Total	25.2%	1.4%	1.5%	6.7%	53.6%	3.6%	0.4%
By Income							
<$10,000	15.7%	2.5%	1.7%	5.8%	62.8%	2.5%	0.8%
$10-20,000	20.1%	0.6%	1.3%	5.2%	61.7%	1.9%	0.6%
$20-30,000	31.5%	0.8%	0.8%	2.4%	55.1%	2.4%	0.8%
$30-50,000	27.5%	1.1%	1.1%	7.9%	47.1%	7.9%	0.0%
$50,000 +	32.8%	2.5%	1.7%	10.1%	42.0%	4.2%	0.0%
Total	25.5%	1.4%	1.3%	6.3%	53.5%	4.1%	0.4%

Table 32. On average how many books do you get a chance to read each year?

Age Group	None	1-4	5-9	10-24	25+
18-24	11.2%	32.2%	23.1%	19.6%	10.5%
25-34	6.9%	25.8%	14.5%	27.7%	17.6%
35-44	10.0%	24.4%	21.1%	30.0%	9.4%
45-54	18.8%	25.0%	18.0%	19.5%	14.1%
55 and above	24.2%	29.7%	13.7%	17.0%	11.0%
Total	14.4%	27.3%	17.7%	23.3%	12.2%
By Income					
<$10,000	24.0%	23.1%	20.7%	18.2%	9.9%
$10-20,000	20.3%	25.5%	13.7%	23.5%	12.4%
$20-30,000	11.1%	31.0%	21.4%	21.4%	9.5%
$30-50,000	9.5%	28.4%	17.4%	26.3%	11.6%
$50,000 +	5.1%	27.1%	21.2%	26.3%	14.4%
Total	13.8%	27.1%	18.5%	23.4%	11.6%

Table 33. How important is religion in your life?

Age Group	Extremely Important	Somewhat Important	Not Important
18-24	59.0%	30.6%	10.4%
25-34	78.6%	15.1%	5.0%
35-44	83.9%	11.7%	4.4%
45-54	85.9%	9.4%	3.9%
55 and above	81.3%	11.0%	6.6%
Total	78.2%	15.2%	6.0%
By Income			
<$10,000	74.6%	22.1%	3.3%
$10-20,000	77.8%	14.4%	7.8%
$20-30,000	76.0%	15.2%	8.0%
$30-50,000	77.2%	16.9%	5.3%
$50,000 +	84.7%	7.6%	5.9%
Total	77.9%	15.4%	6.1%

Table 34a. Do you think the Democratic Party is committed to issues that are most important to blacks?

Age Group	Yes	No	By Income	Yes	No
18–24	53.5%	37.5%	<$10,000	65.6%	24.6%
25–34	61.0%	32.1%	$10–20,000	62.7%	30.7%
35–44	57.5%	34.3%	$20–30,000	61.1%	30.2%
45–54	58.6%	32.0%	$30–50,000	57.7%	34.9%
55 and above	68.1%	23.1%	$50,000 +	54.2%	42.4%
Total	60.1%	31.5%	Total	60.2%	32.6%

Table 34b. Do you think the Republican Party is committed to issues that are most important to blacks?

Age Group	Yes	No	By Income	Yes	No
18–24	8.4%	83.2%	<$10,000	13.2%	74.4%
25–34	12.6%	79.2%	$10–20,000	7.2%	84.3%
35–44	10.6%	81.1%	$20–30,000	9.5%	82.5%
45–54	9.4%	82.7%	$30–50,000	6.3%	88.4%
55 and above	8.3%	82.3%	$50,000 +	10.1%	84.9%
Total	10.0%	81.6%	Total	8.9%	83.5%

Table 35.   Would you describe the role and influence of your local church as the "most important in the community," "one of several influences" or "not a major influence?"

Age Group	Most Important	One of Several	Not Major
18-24	27.8%	36.8%	31.3%
25-34	30.2%	46.5%	20.8%
35-44	29.4%	46.7%	19.4%
45-54	30.7%	44.1%	22.8%
55 and above	40.7%	35.2%	15.4%
Total	32.2%	41.6%	21.3%
By Income			
<$10,000	38.5%	41.0%	15.6%
$10-20,000	36.6%	34.6%	22.2%
$20-30,000	23.8%	46.8%	27.0%
$30-50,000	30.3%	41.5%	24.5%
$50,000 +	21.2%	51.7%	24.6%
Total	30.4%	42.6%	22.9%

Table 36. Would you like to own a business someday?

Age Group	Yes	No	By Income	Yes	No
18-24	79.2%	33.3%	<$10,000	65.3%	33.1%
25-34	83.0%	20.1%	$10-20,000	65.6%	32.5%
35-44	75.6%	15.1%	$20-30,000	71.4%	27.0%
45-54	70.1%	22.8%	$30-50,000	70.9%	28.0%
55 and above	32.6%	29.1%	$50,000 +	69.5%	30.5%
Total	66.8%	31.3%	Total	68.6%	30.1%

Table 37. Which of the following institutions do you think can do the most to improve the situation for black families today?

Age Group	Individuals & Families	Community Organizations	Civil Rights Groups	Churches	Government
18-24	42.4%	18.8%	2.1%	16.7%	16.0%
25-34	55.3%	10.1%	3.1%	19.5%	6.3%
35-44	53.0%	13.3%	5.0%	16.0%	7.2%
45-54	45.7%	11.8%	7.9%	24.4%	7.1%
55 and above	39.4%	16.1%	7.2%	19.4%	11.1%
Total	47.3%	14.0%	5.0%	19.1%	9.5%
By Income					
<$10,000	36.1%	14.8%	3.3%	23.8%	13.1%
$10-20,000	45.8%	15.0%	3.9%	21.6%	11.1%
$20-30,000	47.6%	12.7%	7.1%	17.5%	10.3%
$30-50,000	53.4%	18.0%	2.6%	14.3%	6.9%
$50,000 +	54.2%	9.3%	7.6%	17.8%	5.9%
Total	47.9%	14.4%	4.7%	18.6%	9.3%

Table 38. Is your spouse or partner enrolled in a pension plan other than social security?

Age Group	Yes	No	By Income	Yes	No
18-24	14.0%	84.6%	<$10,000	11.6%	87.6%
25-34	43.1%	55.0%	$10-20,000	25.5%	73.2%
35-44	54.4%	43.9%	$20-30,000	38.1%	59.5%
45-54	50.0%	47.7%	$30-50,000	65.1%	34.9%
55 and above	46.7%	51.6%	$50,000 +	78.8%	21.2%
Total	42.3%	55.7%	Total	44.8%	54.3%

61

Table 39. Excluding the mortgage, about how much debt, if any, do you currently have?

Age Group	None	< $500	$500-1000	$1000-5000	> $5000
18-24	38.2%	12.5%	15.3%	19.4%	11.8%
25-34	11.9%	5.0%	15.1%	27.7%	34.0%
35-44	8.3%	6.1%	15.0%	25.6%	36.7%
45-54	4.7%	4.7%	10.2%	28.1%	47.7%
55 and above	22.5%	7.7%	13.7%	18.1%	28.0%
Total	17.0%	7.2%	13.8%	23.3%	31.5%
By Income					
<$10,000	37.2%	10.7%	14.0%	17.4%	19.0%
$10-20,000	19.6%	8.5%	20.9%	26.8%	22.9%
$20-30,000	8.0%	6.4%	13.6%	40.0%	30.4%
$30-50,000	9.0%	6.9%	14.4%	25.0%	43.6%
$50,000 +	11.0%	3.4%	11.0%	21.2%	49.2%
Total	16.3%	7.2%	15.0%	26.1%	33.5%

Table 40. Do you think you will be financially better off, worse off or as well off as your parents?

Age Group	Better	Worse off	As Well off
18-24	75.0%	1.4%	23.6%
25-34	73.0%	5.0%	20.1%
35-44	69.4%	10.0%	17.2%
45-54	62.2%	11.0%	25.2%
55 and above	77.3%	5.0%	12.7%
Total	71.8%	6.5%	19.1%
By Income			
<$10,000	55.7%	9.8%	30.3%
$10-20,000	69.9%	7.2%	20.3%
$20-30,000	77.0%	6.3%	15.1%
$30-50,000	73.3%	5.3%	20.1%
$50,000 +	87.3%	2.5%	10.2%
Total	33.6%	20.3%	41.1%

Table 41.   Do you expect to get married some day or not?

Age Group	Yes	No	By Income	Yes	No
18-24	81.7%	13.5%	<$10,000	48.0%	43.9%
25-34	73.6%	19.8%	$10-20,000	54.5%	39.7%
35-44	59.8%	33.0%	$20-30,000	58.5%	35.4%
45-54	33.9%	56.5%	$30-50,000	67.0%	29.2%
55 and above	20.2%	70.2%	$50,000 +	61.4%	22.7%
Total	56.6%	35.9%	Total	57.4%	35.7%

Table 42.   How worried are you personally of contracting HIV, the virus that causes AIDS?

Age Group	Very Worried	Somewhat Worried	Not too Worried	Already HIV Positive
18-24	24.3%	20.1%	54.9%	0.0%
25-34	20.1%	8.8%	67.9%	0.0%
35-44	12.8%	13.3%	72.2%	0.6%
45-54	16.4%	6.3%	75.0%	0.0%
55 and above	4.4%	5.5%	85.6%	0.0%
Total	15.0%	10.6%	71.7%	0.2%
By Income				
<$10,000	20.5%	11.5%	66.4%	0.0%
$10-20,000	24.2%	11.8%	64.1%	0.0%
$20-30,000	16.0%	12.0%	70.4%	0.8%
$30-50,000	10.5%	6.8%	82.6%	0.0%
$50,000 +	5.9%	11.0%	82.2%	0.0%
Total	15.4%	10.3%	73.6%	0.1%

Survey Methodology

This national telephone poll of a random sample of 800 black adults was conducted for the National Urban League by Blum & Weprin Associates, Inc. April 1-17, 2001. The sample was based on an RDD design which draws numbers from telephone exchanges in all 50 states, giving all phone numbers, listed and unlisted, a proportionate chance of being included. Respondents were selected randomly within the household, and then screened for race. The sample was quotaed by region. Results were weighted by gender and age to reflect the most recent U.S. Census estimates of the black adult population. The estimated average sample tolerance for data is $\pm$ 3.5 percent at the 95 percent confidence level. That is, the chances are about 19 out of 20 that if all black households with telephones were surveyed with the same questionnaire, the results of the complete census would not be found to deviate from the poll findings by more than 3.5 percentage points. Error for subgroups is higher.

The Rules of the Game
(If you think the old rules still apply, you're in denial)

BY SHERYL HUGGINS

You can't change the world if you refuse to acknowledge the forces that are already shaping it. For years, alarmists have decried the "decline" in our society (e.g., too many single mothers, not enough leaders), but they've missed the point. While they were sounding the alarm, society as we knew it did fall apart, and now it's being rebuilt according to new ethos, attitudes and conventions. I've written the following not as a manifesto for how things should be, but as a wake-up call about how they actually are to a new generation of Americans.

RACE: We finally admit that race is a political construct and begin to fashion our identities around heritage.

POLITICS: Party loyalty is out; identity politics are in.

ACTIVISM: No one will settle for second-class citizenship and double standards; no one's asking for permission to be equal anymore.

FAMILY: Family structures accommodate our lives, not the other way around. Quit whining about the destruction of the family, because the old system died a long time ago (we've just been in denial) and we're in uncharted territory now. Deal with it.

CAREER: No one expects a lifetime career and everyone wants to be his or her own boss. Security is a myth, so get over it.

ROMANCE & SEXUALITY: No guarantees, no compromises, take no prisoners. Pursue a sense of good self-esteem and you can't go wrong.

COMMUNITY: It's about common interests, not geography. Formalized interaction is out the window; everything's personal and casual.

HEALTH: Good health is earned, not inherited.

BEAUTY: Beauty standards are more diverse and with discipline (or money), you too can be beautiful.

FINANCES: Don't expect big brother to take care of you, because you're on your own. And you can't take it with you, so spend it, baby.

TECHNOLOGY: It's a personal, empowering force, not a dehumanizing force that will crush you, then replace you. Mastering it is the key to success.

COMMUNICATION: Get to the point and make it convenient—all the time.

RELIGION: It's personal, as opposed to communal.

HERO WORSHIP: The aristocracy's reign is dead. Celebrity and notoriety rule, and the line between the two is often blurred.

SUCCESS: Being known is the ultimate form of success.

A Tale of Two Classes: The Socio-Economic Divide Among Black Americans Under 35

BY CELESTE M. WATKINS[1]

For one segment of the generation of African Americans under 35, the current era is the best of times. Credentialed with college as well as graduate- and professional-school degrees, skilled in the use of the latest technological wizardry, possessed of the "right" jobs with the "right" potential, and supported by competitive salaries, they have benefited enormously from the expanded opportunity American society now offers more and more African Americans—and they readily express the self-confidence such success breeds.

But what is the apt characterization of the current era for the other segment of African Americans under 35?

For this group—who are not credentialed with higher education degrees, and thus, who are not a part of the heady swirl of the white-collar world; who may not have even high school diplomas, or, if they do, have neither the education nor the training that would make those diplomas meaningful; who are consigned now to the low-wage service jobs of the economy, if they have a job at all—the right words or phrases are far more difficult to select.

For the latter group, is the current era a new beginning, a climb out of the material and psychological swamp of continual un- and underemployment? The sharp, quick decline in the black unem-

ployment rate in the late 1990s, powered by many of the so-called
hard-core unemployed taking the low-wage service jobs the booming economy offered, showed that most of those in this profoundly
disparaged cohort know all about the value of work, want to work,
and will whenever they are given a chance.

Will they now, in the period when the air is thick with job cut-
backs among American companies and foreboding about a recession, still be given a chance?

Or will the American economy return to its old "tradition" of
not just double-digit black unemployment, but high double-digit
black unemployment?

And if that happens, what will Black America do?

This issue—the future of those in their generation who have
had relatively little opportunity—is the most critical question
under-35 African Americans face. For the ways in which blacks of
different socioeconomic groups seek to deal with and help each
other will, in large measure, determine the future economic, social,
and political health of Black America itself.

Despite both the appearance and the reality of a growing class
divide among this segment of Black America, both groups, those
who have great access to opportunity and those who have little,
need for each other to do well if Black America as a whole is to
prosper.

How will we respond to this dilemma? The growing class
divide confronts Black America's rising leadership with one of its
most serious challenges.

It is not, of course, as if class divisions are something new to
Black America. What are new, however, are their scope and the
forces behind it. When William Julius Wilson argued this very point
in his groundbreaking 1978 book *The Declining Significance of Race*,
asserting that the life chances of individual African Americans have
more to do with their economic class positions than their day-to-
day encounters with racism, he faced a wave of criticisms.[2] Class

had rarely been such a focus for scholars studying blacks in America. The suggestion of its prominence caused some to worry that Wilson was arguing that middle-class blacks had by and large "made it" and no longer faced the challenges of racism. Many scholars, public intellectuals, and political pundits challenged Wilson to defend his contention and to address the questions—how much did class really matter for the experiences of African Americans and what were the implications of this notion?

Years later, Wilson's argument is less controversial. In fact, it is taken as a widely agreed upon thesis by scholars and non-scholars alike. Social scientists point out the widening class gap within the African-American community as income inequality increases across all American households. They highlight the implications of such a gap in terms of varying access to education, jobs, and the networks that can lead to socioeconomic mobility. Others, particularly blacks themselves, notice the gap as well, often in the diversity of class pre-sentation in public spaces and within African-American familial net-works. From behind the fast-food counters to within black corporate elite circles, many African Americans are paying attention to the variation in opportunities and life experiences of members of their communities. They are discussing privately and publicly how to best understand and respond to the class-based differences within contemporary Black America because they realize that these differ-ences can potentially strain the political limits of racial solidarity.

While the condition of poorer blacks has occupied social scien-tists for decades, increased attention is now being paid to the expe-riences of working-class, middle-class, and upper-class blacks. These more precise ways of defining the experiences of African-Americans have led to at least three conclusions. First, as Wilson argued, the opportunities and experiences of African Americans heavily depend on their class status.[3] Second, within the black community, the gap is indeed widening between the "haves" and the "have-nots." Third, such a widening gap has major implications for the interclass relations of blacks as well as for the broader poli-cy agenda of the African-American community.[4]

The Development of the Divide: The Evolution of Class in Black America

In pre-industrial America, while mobility was largely limited by racial subjugation, blacks occupied differing social and econom-ic positions in a truncated class system. The position that one main-tained depended largely on his or her relationship to the institution of slavery. Slaves, depending on the location and size of the plan-tation and whether they worked primarily in the fields or in the homes of their masters, had varying experiences that would have major implications for their potential socioeconomic mobility after slavery. Working in slaveowner homes, on smaller plantations, or in more heavily populated urban areas tended to afford slaves with more occasions to learn some of the habits and skills of those who maintained much of the country's political and economic control. Once free, many of these slaves, along with other free blacks, sub-sisted mainly on farming, real estate, artisanship, and small busi-ness ownership, with a few accumulating some amount of wealth.[5]

W. E. B. DuBois' *The Philadelphia Negro* highlighted how, lured by the promise of economic opportunity, large numbers of African Americans migrated from the agrarian South to northern cities shortly after slavery ended.[6] This migration created tension for an already delicate configuration of blacks that resided often in racial-ly mixed areas in northern cities before, and immediately follow-ing, Emancipation.[7] As the migration trend increased during the Industrial Revolution of the early 1900s, many African Americans, finding limited opportunity and increased competition from work-ing-class whites and immigrant groups, were systematically shut out of the labor market and left to fend for themselves in segregat-ed communities.[8]

Limited economic, political, and social opportunities provided fertile ground for the intergenerational reproduction of poverty and social problems such as crime, poor education, family instability, and violence in many African-American communities. Segregation encouraged the interaction of classes within the black community and served to offset some of the effects of the systematic economic and political disempowerment of blacks. Black business owners, doctors and other professionals serviced predominately, and often exclusively, black clientele.[9] Poorer blacks often lived in the same or in close-by neighborhoods to blacks that were more affluent. While the income of many blacks was derived almost solely from black clientele, others challenged the hegemonic arrangements that kept them out of the industrial economy, eventually opening access for blacks to many of the jobs that provided economic stability and potential socioeconomic mobility. By the mid-1900s that challenge included increasingly successful efforts to wrest their share of local political power out of the hands of predominately white political machines.

However, class tensions did exist within these communities as psychologist Kenneth Clark and other scholars have noted.[10] Class tension, regardless of race, persists in America and has since the country's inception. Sharing a common racial history, however, added a distinct complexity to the relationships of blacks across class lines. First, the proposed means by which African Americans should pursue economic, social, and political equality with the rest of America often differed along class lines as some pushed for full racial integration while others prescribed building economic power through racial solidarity.[11] Second, with so many African Americans relegated to the lowest rungs on the job ladder or shut out completely from the labor market, neighborhood instability challenged the desires of many to have communities that encouraged upward mobility and integration into the economic, political, and social realms of the larger society. Third, class diversity within black families meant that numerous African Americans faced the fact that some of those who challenged community norms were members of their own families.

Following World War II, large structural changes in the economy had major implications for the American class structure, affecting the African-American community significantly. In fact, the largest changes in black mobility occurred in the 1950s and 1960s. Increases in African-American employment in the government and private sector, sparked by the passage of the Fair Employment Practices Act and the economic expansion after the war, sharply increased the size of the African-American working and middle classes.[12] By the 1970s, some suburban communities opened to African Americans, allowing the more affluent members of predominately African-American neighborhoods to move. In addition, increased economic opportunity through the gains of the Civil Rights Movement and affirmative action programs gave many African Americans increased opportunities to solidify their positions in the American middle class.

At the same time, however, economic shifts and public policies in the 1970s and 1980s intensified the stressful economic situation of the inner-city communities where many lower and some working-class blacks remained. Hit hard by economic recessions and inflation, poverty rates for the nation's central cities rose from 12.7 percent to 19 percent between 1969 and 1985.[13] Starting in mid-1970s, the poverty rate for children of all ethnic groups rose, with African-American children disproportionately represented in this trend. Many scholars have linked the rise in child poverty with the increase in female-headed households. By 1995, 63 percent of all black children were in female-headed households, and 46 percent of black female-headed households were in poverty.[14] Further, as Wilson argues in *The Truly Disadvantaged*, the decline in real wages, structural joblessness in the inner city, and the increase in income inequality struck inner-city African-American communities particularly hard.

Throughout the 1990s, scholars and journalists paid increased attention to those at the bottom of the economic ladder in their writings. Terms such as "the underclass" and "ghetto poor" were used to describe those inhabiting the core of America's central cities who, for the most part, had been shut out of the technological and economic advances of the past decades.[15] This group had evolved as a result of current and historic discrimination, the dynamics of the low-wage labor market, the decentralization of businesses, middle- and working-class outmigration, un- and underemployment, and limited education and skills. These macrostructural changes were linked to the concentration of poverty in inner cities as well as the rise in black female-headed families, out-of-wedlock births, and crime. Experiencing long-term spells of poverty and welfare receipt, this group was a small segment of the low-income African-American families residing in inner cities, yet received major attention by scholars and policy makers alike.[16]

The result of all of these forces and developments is a more variegated class structure within Black America, with each stratum facing similar but often distinct challenges. In 1998, 26 percent of African Americans (9.1 million) were living in poverty, compared with 8 percent of non-Hispanic whites (15.8 million).[17] The condition of the black lower class and ghetto poor persists, with scholars fine-tuning their understanding of and policy prescriptions for this group, composed of not only the chronically un- and underemployed but also the working poor. The working poor, as highlighted by anthropologist Katherine Newman, are employed, yet still poor due to low wages, limited benefits, few opportunities for mobility, and increased competition as additional workers enter the labor market through welfare reform and a booming economy.[18] Others are raising questions about the challenges, mobility and opportunities of working-class blacks, situated between a lower class with whom they often share communities and a middle class whose position may be precarious.

Scholars and journalists have also raised concerns about the actual economic and political power of the black middle class and have highlighted that while the black-white income gap may be decreasing, the wealth gap remains sizable.[19] In addition, while African Americans have gained political power in central cities, the surrounding, predominantly-white suburban areas have continued to attract both businesses and residents, challenging the influence that these localities can wield.[20] In 1999, while the median income of African-American households was $27,910, the highest ever recorded, it still significantly trailed the $44,366 median income of white non-Hispanic households.[21]

Yet, one cannot deny that, at the same time, African Americans have gained significant ground on both economic and political fronts. Drops in the unemployment rate, poverty rate, and welfare participation have suggested that low-income blacks have benefited from the economy of the mid- to late 1990s. More and more blacks have become a part of the nation's political life through public service in elected and appointed positions. In 1999, about 47 percent of African-American householders were homeowners.[22] As Orlando Patterson highlights, middle-class African-Americans now own more businesses, control a greater share of the national income, and head more corporations than at any other period.[23] In fact, about 6.1 percent of black households had annual incomes over $100,000 in 1999.[24]

The Widening Class Gap: Issues & Complications

Income inequality in America increased steadily between 1967 and the early 1990s, tapering slightly around 1992. In 1999, the household at the 95th percentile received $142,021 in income, 8.3 times that of the household at the 20th percentile ($17,196). In 1967, this ratio was 6.3. For African-American households, in 1999, the household at the 95th percentile received $106,800 in income, 10.1 times that of the household at the 20th percentile ($10,626). In

1967, this ratio was 7.6.[25] In other words, while income inequality has grown for all American households and has been slightly higher for black households throughout the decades, the gap has recently grown even wider for black households.

Is a widening class gap among African Americans necessarily problematic? Some would argue that because income inequality is rising across American households, the gap should not be a concern. In fact, some would argue that such inequality is simply further evidence that the trends for blacks are becoming more in line with the trends for the rest of society. Perhaps such a gap will encourage those African Americans on the bottom of the economic ladder to strive for mobility as they see more and more blacks taking their places on the higher rungs. Certainly, those at the top of the ladder should be encouraged to dismantle the truncated class structure in the black economic sphere and to climb to the upper echelons of the American class system.

While these points are well taken, a widening class gap within Black America presents similar problems as rising income inequality cross all American households. While class mobility may be a beneficial and favorable goal, when that mobility occurs only for those already on the higher rungs of the economic ladder, intractable inequality rises. Inequality of outcomes (in this case, income) on the surface may not be a problem. However, in American society, too often inequality of outcomes leads to and reinforces inequality of opportunities, creating not a class system but a caste-like one. As some climb to the top, others will be left on the bottom with very few opportunities for upward mobility and a future so bleak that deprivation, particularly in a land of wealth, could potentially lead to desperation.

African Americans under 35 must forcefully come to grips with this issue. The reason is that although the problem is not new, they have come of age in an American society in which they have opportunities to compose their racial identities at a time of largely implicit rather than explicit racial tension. While racism is still very much a part of this generation's consciousness and overall life experiences, its often subtle manifestations in the members' daily experiences has enabled some to create political consciousness that may not hinge entirely on racial solidarity. Many note the class gap and wrestle with it in their daily encounters with African Americans higher and lower on the socioeconomic ladder. Many even think about it when engaging in dialogue about the future leadership needs of Black America. How does one represent the interests of a social group whose issues and objectives seem increasingly diverse and at times, in opposition to each other? There is a lack of clarity on how best to respond to the class gap, both on a broader community level and in the day-to-day interactions of blacks across class lines. Two complications are central.

First, many African Americans want to live in socioeconomically diverse black neighborhoods. But their desire is often sapped by the instability that pervades neighborhoods with significant numbers of poor residents. The resulting internal conflict frequently ends with those better-off opting for less economically diverse communities that wholeheartedly encourage upward mobility.[26] Social scientists Katherine Newman, Elijah Anderson, and Mary Pattillo-McCoy all highlight these tensions in neighborhoods whose members represent not only varying class positions but also different ways of thinking about the appropriate values and norms for their communities. At the same time, those with limited opportunities for advancement are often frustrated by the perceived lack of ongoing support and resources afforded by more successful members of the community. Sharing these neighborhoods, in the face of rising income inequality, has highlighted the diversity of economic and political ideologies and agendas, ideas about the presentation of self in public spaces, and methods of protest, challenging those in these communities to consider the degree to which these things should be policed or embraced.

Second, because of their history in this country, African Americans have a shared desire for economic, social, and political equality with the rest of America. However, some blacks are closer than others to achieving this goal, raising the question of whether the means by which this goal is to be pursued should be the same throughout the black community. A further question is whether there is enough opportunity in American capitalist society to lift up the remaining segment of Black America. Largely through racial integration, blacks, particularly those under 35, are faced with the fact that their experiences—professional, educational and cultural—are often vastly different from others sharing their racial, but not socioeconomic, class backgrounds. In fact, depending on their backgrounds, some blacks would argue that in certain aspects, they have more in common with some of their white counterparts than with blacks of a different socioeconomic class. While finding common ground is important, many are realizing that the diversity of interests, ideologies, and ways of being within the black community may not lead, nor should they necessarily lead, to the same strategies for responding to racial and economic subordination.

Bridging the Divide: Strategies & Directives for the Under 35 Generation

It is imperative to respond to the socioeconomic divide on both intra- and interracial levels. The former must take place largely through the interpersonal interactions of people of diverse socioeconomic groups. The latter must take place through a broader political agenda that is sensitive to the socioeconomic diversity within Black America.

Interclass relations

Increased class-based tension is certainly an understandable—indeed, unavoidable—by-product of rising income inequality within the black community. In his book *Harlemworld: Doing Race and Class in Contemporary Black America*, anthropologist John L. Jackson argues that it is problematic, however, to think of Black America as two overtly discrete worlds—one lower class, one middle class—that rarely, if ever, interact in meaningful ways. While black suburban flight has encouraged geographic distance between blacks of different classes, there are often opportunities through familial ties, churches and other institutions, and in shared public spaces, for blacks to interact across class lines, mitigating some of this social distance.[27]

In order to respond to potential tensions, at least three actions are necessary, particularly from the generation of 25-35 year old African Americans poised to become leaders in their communities. First, there must be a cross-pollination of resources through familial ties, churches and other community organizations, and opportunities created by individuals. Research suggests that often what encourages mobility, and the behaviors necessary for mobility, are social networks that are extensive and diverse. These network connections need not be strong relationships; in fact, jobs and other opportunities often come because of "weak ties," knowing a friend of a friend or having brief contact with someone who passes along important information.[28] The value of this cross-pollination cannot be underestimated in the development of relationships and resources to bridge the socioeconomic divide.

Second, there must be a fundamental acceptance among black people of their own diversity and, to borrow from Jackson, of different ways of "doing blackness" within the African-American community. Questioning racial authenticity due to political views, socioeconomic status, or presentation of self is futile at best. Of course, it is imperative for us to hold ourselves accountable for our actions. Questioning behaviors and views is important and challenges the notion of blacks as a monolithic group. Furthermore, it is a universal human trait to categorize and draw boundaries to make sense of our social worlds. Thus, one cannot expect African Americans to not make use of those categories, boundaries, and social measuring sticks to distinguish themselves from other blacks. We should not be dismayed that it happens. However, we must try mightily to not allow personal animus to derail the exchange of resources, information, and ideas across class lines.

Third, it is imperative for African Americans to be involved in debates that shape the political and economic future of this country. Allowing a diversity of views encourages creative, achievable, and effective approaches to responding to what ultimately perpetuates much of the class gap in America—inequality of opportunity. This kind of inequality is often inextricably linked not only to economic stagnation but many of the behaviors that threaten the labor force participation and family and neighborhood stability of many in this country. Power in America is largely gained through economic resources obtained through education, ownership, and networks. Many blacks have obtained, or are on their way to obtaining, this power on an individual level. Whether presented as a collective agenda by civil rights organizations and leaders or as several different views by a variety of individuals, the ability to leverage power allows one to sit at the table when decisions facing the nation are made. As a larger heterogeneity of social and political views of African Americans come to the forefront, it is possible to garner broad support for some initiatives among African Americans yet respect and appreciate those times when there is little opportunity to gather support simply on the basis of racial solidarity. Similarly, there is great potential to build multi-racial coalitions around some issues, using this power to create initiatives that while not race-based, respond to the widening class gap within Black America and improve the conditions of blacks in this country.[29]

Toward a Broader Political Agenda

First, it is important to remember that the class gap within Black America is not just the black community's problem. It is America's problem. Just as affluent African Americans should be encouraged to consider their responsibilities toward less affluent blacks, it is also essential to challenge those forces in American society that created and sustain widening income inequality in America. After all, those large reservoirs of low-wage workers who are poorly educated were not created by black elites. These reservoirs are the product of decades of systematic racial subjugation—and that is a problem for which America as a whole bears responsibility.

Second, policies designed to increase and sustain labor force participation can greatly assist those on the bottom third of the socioeconomic class structure. As seen in the recent presidential election, issues facing low-income households have not taken center stage. Yet the current threat of an economic recession reminds us of the needs of this group who are particularly affected by shifts in the economy. Policies that encourage us to make work pay through the Earned Income Tax Credit, living wages, and family friendly employment benefits assist all low-income families and greatly assist families in the bottom third of the black economic class structure. African-American leaders should not ignore these policies and others like it such as the recent changes to the welfare policy. Further, it is imperative that there be increased dialogue and initiatives to directly address the increasing incarceration of a disproportionate number of blacks and other people of color, eliminating many future labor force opportunities, breaking up families, and disenfranchising a large number of people once released. Finally, the recent increase in participation in the low-wage labor market due to the booming economy and welfare reform reminds us that the black hard-core unemployed have shown that by and large they will respond vigorously to the opportunity to work. This underscores the continuing need for creative, yet cost effective ways to improve the skill level of workers through education and training, for fairer housing policy for poorer Americans, and for public and private health insurance that covers low-income families. As Wilson argues, there is great potential for multi-racial coalition building around these issues as they potentially benefit all lower- and working-class Americans.[30]

Third, we must support policies that allow working- and middle-class Americans to secure assets and build wealth, which would greatly aid African Americans in these socioeconomic groups. Policy conversations often focus on the needs of lower-class and middle-class Americans. Working-class Americans then, find themselves attracted to demands for education and training, affordable health care, and community development attractive to low-income families as well as home ownership policies, entrepreneurship opportunities, and wealth building incentives attractive to the middle class. These kinds of policy initiatives have major implications for the economic stability and mobility of black households and many of them, because they appeal across racial lines, have great potential for garnering widespread political support.

Fourth, the transmission of wealth intergenerationally positions African Americans to solidify and improve upon their economic standing and to reduce wealth inequality within the American socioeconomic class structure. In her book *Black Picket Fences*, Mary Pattillo-McCoy describes the difficulty that some members of the black middle class have passing their class position on to their children compared to their white middle-class counterparts.[31] Further, Oliver & Shapiro in *Black Wealth, White Wealth* highlight the disparities of wealth between racial groups, suggesting a potentially tenuous position for middle- and upper-class blacks.[32] Through initiatives designed to educate households on how to not only build but pass on wealth, African-Americans could solidify the economic gains made in the past several years and position themselves to eliminate the wealth gap between themselves and their white counterparts.

Conclusion

In this article, I highlighted several of the important issues around the widening socioeconomic class gap among African-American households. Tracing the evolution of this divide, I have historically grounded the debate, demonstrating that while class has always been salient within the African-American community, the recently widened income gap along with the unprecedented position of blacks under 35 have created new challenges. With these class-based variations of life experiences have come a wide array of ideologies, ideas, and agendas around economic and political empowerment, the definitions of a "black community" and the values therein, and the complications around intra-race relations across class lines. I presented a two-tier approach. One includes an intra-racial focus on the interpersonal interactions of people of diverse socioeconomic groups. The other stresses an interracial push for a broader political agenda that is sensitive to the socioeconomic diversity within Black America and encourages Wilson's prescription for multi-racial coalition building. Both of these approaches create solutions that are sensitive to the diversity—economic, political, and cultural—within Black America.

Notes

[1] Watkins is currently a Ph.D. candidate in the Sociology department at Harvard University and a fellow in the Harvard Multidisciplinary Program in Inequality and Social Policy. Watkins' areas of research interest include urban poverty; formal organizations; social policy; and race, class, and gender. Her dissertation investigates organizational dynamics in welfare offices. The author expresses her special gratitude to Katherine Newman, William Julius Wilson, John L. Jackson & Laurel Beatty for their comments and criticisms on earlier drafts of this paper. None of the above should be held responsible for or presumed to agree with the argument of this article.

[2] Wilson, William Julius. 1978. *The Declining Significance of Race: Blacks & Changing American Institutions.* Chicago: University of Chicago Press.

[3] The definitions and criteria for socioeconomic class status are diverse. Most scholars use some combination of education, income, occupation, and wealth to measure it. For the purposes of this article, I use a definition that focuses primarily on income.

[4] This assumes that African-Americans in this country constitute a social group and therefore have a collective interest in the progress of all members.

[5] For more discussion of this, see E. Franklin Frazier's *The Black Bourgeoisie* (1957) New York: The Free Press.

[6] Du Bois, W.E.B. 1996ed. *The Philadelphia Negro*. Philadelphia: U Penn Press.

[7] Wilson, 1978.

[8] Allan Spear points out in the 1971 article "The Origins of the Urban Ghetto, 1870-1915," that Black enclaves existed in New York, Chicago, and Washington since early in the 19th century. However, increased migration from the South during WWI, the 1920s and WWII accelerated the formation of urban ghettos. Article published in *Key Issues in the Afro-American Experience* edited by Higgins, Kilson & Fox. New York: Harcourt Brace Jovanovich, Inc. For discussion of the economic competition between African Americans and immigrant groups during the Industrial Revolution, see Lieberson's 1980 book *A Piece of the Pie: Blacks & White Immigrants Since 1880*. Berkeley: University of California Press.

[9] Landry, Bart. 1987. *The New Black Middle Class*. Berkeley: University of California Press.

[10] Clark, Kenneth. 1965. *Dark Ghetto: Dilemmas of Social Power*. New York: Harper & Row. See also Ulf Hannerz's 1969 *Soulside: Inquiries Into Ghetto Life & Culture*. New York: Columbia University Press & Katherine Newman's 1992 article "Culture & Structure in *The Truly Disadvantaged*." City & Society. 6(1): 3-25.

[11] For a more detailed discussion of this, see John Hope Franklin & August Meier's 1982 edited volume, *Black Leaders of the Twentieth Century*. Urbana: University of Illinois Press.

[12] For a more detailed discussion of this, see Wilson 1978.

[13] Harris, Fred & Roger Wilkins. 1988. *Quiet Riots: Race & Poverty in the United States*. New York: Pantheon Books

[14] U.S. Census Bureau. 1996. *The Black Population in the United States*, March 1995. Washington, DC: On-line data. While the number of babies born to married women began to fall starting in the late 1960s, after 1975, the number of babies born to unmarried women of all racial groups began to rise. With divorce becoming more common, the fraction of women raising children without men in the home also increased. However, this trend has particularly affected African-American families. For a more detailed discussion of this, see Orlando Patterson's 1997 *The Ordeal of Integration: Progress and Resentment in America's "Racial" Crisis*. Washington, DC: Civitas.

[15] Wilson, William Julius. 1987. *The Truly Disadvantaged: The Inner City, the Underclass, & Public Policy*. Chicago: University of Chicago Press. Jencks,

Christopher & Paul Peterson. 1991. *The Urban Underclass*. Washington, DC: Brookings Institution. Gans, Herbert. 1995. *The War Against the Poor: The Underclass & Anti-Poverty Policy*. New York: Basic Books.

[16] It is difficult to quantify the "underclass" because scholars use varying definitions and criteria. In fact, largely because scholars dispute its definition and because of the political controversy around the use of the term, most scholars and journalists are reluctant to still use it.

[17] The poverty rate of blacks has declined from a high of 38 percent in 1969. U.S. Census Bureau. 2000. *The Black Population in the United States*, March 1999. Washington, DC: On-line data.

[18] See Newman, Katherine. 1999. *No Shame in My Game: The Working Poor in the Inner City*. New York: Knopf & Russell Sage.

[19] Oliver, Melvin L. & Thomas M. Shapiro. 1995. *Black Wealth/White Wealth: A New Perspective on Racial Inequality*. New York: Routledge. Conley, Dalton. 1999. *Being Black, Living in the Red: Race, Wealth, & Social Policy in America*. Berkeley: University of California Press.

[20] See Wilson 1978 for a more in-depth explanation of this.

[21] U.S. Census Bureau. 2000. *Money Income in the United States: 1999*. Current Population Reports, P60-209. U.S. Government Printing Office. Washington, DC.

[22] U.S. Census Bureau 2001. *Report on Residential Vacancies & Homeownership*. Press Release. Washington, DC.

[23] Patterson, 1997.

[24] U.S. Census Bureau. 2000. *Money Income in the United States: 1999*. Current Population Reports, P60-209. U.S. Government Printing Office. Washington, DC.

[25] U.S. Census Bureau. 2000. *Money Income in the United States: 1999*. Current Population Reports, P60-209. U.S. Government Printing Office. Washington, DC.

[26] Anderson, Elijah. 1990. *Streetwise: Race, Class, & Change in an Urban Community*. Chicago: University of Chicago Press. Anderson, Elijah. 1999. *Code of the Street: Decency, Violence, & the Moral Life of the Inner City*. New York: W.W. Norton. Newman, 1999. Pattillo-McCoy, Mary. 1999. *Black Picket Fences: Privilege and Peril Among the Black Middle Class*. Chicago: University of Chicago Press.

[27] Jackson, John L. forthcoming. *Harlemworld: Doing Race & Class in Contemporary Black America*. Chicago: University of Chicago Press.

[28] Granovetter, Mark S. 1973. "The Strength of Weak Ties." *American Journal of Sociology*. 78(6): 1360-1380.

[29] See Wilson, William Julius. 1999. *The Bridge Over the Racial Divide: Rising Inequality & Coalition Politics*. Berkeley: University of California Press.

[30] Wilson, 1999.

[31] Pattillo-McCoy, 1999.

[32] Oliver & Shapiro, 1995.

The Struggle Continues: Race, Equity and Affirmative Action in U.S. Higher Education

BY WALTER R. ALLEN

The American Dream lies at the very heart of the American cultural ethos, and at its center is the emphatic conviction that, in this society, education opens the door to success. Because talent is significantly equated with high educational performance and attainment, the cherished belief that even the poorest American can, with hard work and determination, achieve greatness is a linchpin of the belief that education is the foundation of democracy (Hochschild, 1995). African Americans, despite the stereotypes of them as lazy, ignorant and mentally inferior, have embraced these beliefs to the extreme. Long before the end of the Slave Era, when slaves were threatened with death or severe injury for learning to read and write, blacks invested education with mythic qualities, seeing it as their hope and salvation. They continued to do so after Emancipation—even as White America was developing an elaborate system of institutional barriers to deny African Americans opportunities for schooling. Thus, the Holy Grails of Education in general and of Higher Education in particular have always embodied the broad hopes and frustrations of a people seeking the "promised land" (Allen & Jewell, 1995).

Educational progress in this broad struggle is progress that has come in fits and starts, interspersed with rollbacks and lost ground

(Allen & Jewell, 1995). From 1965 to 1995, equal opportunity programs, and later affirmative action programs, brought hope and promise, and real gains, to the disenfranchised. For a relatively brief moment, this society opened the doors of opportunity and groups previously excluded from key positions and institutions— blacks, Latinos, Asian Americans, and white women—rushed in in significant massive numbers.

Under the imperatives of equity, inclusiveness and diversity, these universities brought in African Americans from such places as the tobacco fields of North Carolina, the Newark ghettoes, the California orchards, and the Saginaw foundries. Equal opportunity and affirmative action programs gave blacks, people of color, women and others routinely pushed to society's fringes, not a guarantee of success, but the chance to compete and the opportunity to succeed.

Now, of course precisely because they've proven their value and effectiveness—because they promise to continue to make significant inroads against the established status quos of racial and patriarchal hierarchy—affirmative action programs are under severe, extensive attack from powerful vested interests.

Affirmative Action in Higher Education

California led the charge to roll back affirmative action. The chief front man for the effort both in California and nationally is an African-American black man who readily admits that he was a beneficiary of affirmative action programs. In the last decade, however, as chair of the University of California Board of Regents, Ward Connerly has worked assiduously to deny similar benefits to black and Latino students. He served as then-Governor Pete Wilson's point man to institute a ban on the use of race as factors in college admissions and the awarding of contracts throughout the university system; then helped engineer voter approval of the so-called "California Civil Rights Initiative," which made it state policy. Connerly and his ideological confreres said, variously, that affirmative action had served its purpose and is no longer necessary; or that it's "reverse discrimination" against guiltless whites; or, the old standby, that the poor and disenfranchised best learn to pull themselves up by their own boot straps. None of these counter-arguments is satisfactory or sufficient. Indeed, their advocates' cynicism and duplicity is apparent in the scrupulous way they ignore other forms of affirmative action in higher education that continue to benefit whites disproportionately—such as preferential treatment for children of alumni, Veteran's preferences, varsity athletes, those who've been privately tutored via standardized test and college application preparation services, and so on.

Affirmative action programs, and their predecessor equal opportunity programs—dramatically expanded opportunity in American society by destroying barriers that systematically prevented the full participation of blacks, people of color and women. Unfortunately, the outcomes of their adoption have been skewed; white women have by far been the greatest beneficiaries of affirmative action. They increased their enrollment by 26 percent between 1978 and 1994, compared to increases of 1 percent for African Americans, 3.6 percent for Asian Americans, and 2.9 percent for Chicano/Latino Americans (Wilson, 1998).

President Johnson's executive order mandating affirmative action sought to eliminate the twin legacies of slavery and Jim Crow—historic and contemporary racial oppression—that kept the substantial mass of blacks mired in poverty and despair (Johnson, 1965).

He invoked the powerful metaphor of a people in chains for 350 years being required to race another people who were and had been free of restraints. Thus, Johnson declared, it wasn't enough in 1965 to merely unchain African Americans and declare the competition an even one from that point on. "You do not take a person who, for years, has been hobbled by chains and liberate him, bring him up to the starting line of a race and then say, 'You are free to compete with all the others,' and still justly believe that you have been completely fair," (Johnson, 1965).

Johnson's executive order called for vigorous, proactive steps—affirmative action—to broaden and increase access to previously excluded, underrepresented groups. Absent extraordinary efforts, American institutions would continue to do "business as usual,"—to restrict the opportunities for access and success of African Americans and other people of color. Equal opportunity legislation and policies evolved into "affirmative action" policies.

However, in this instance the subordinate, degraded status of African Americans was stood on its head: Since the U.S. racial caste system was structured to situate whites at the top and blacks at the bottom (other groups were arranged between these poles based on skin color, physical features, U.S. geo-political interests, culture, etc.), a paradoxical national consensus arose from the majority of "other" Americans. It declared that "what you would do for the *least* of us (i.e., blacks), you most certainly should do for the *rest* of us." Thus, affirmative action's scope and parameters were broadened to include white women, Asians, Latinos, the physically impaired and others.

This shift signaled the eventual *redefinition* of affirmative action away from being a legal remedy or legal compensation for a distinct history of legally sanctioned racial discrimination to the less-morally-powerful status of a mere tool for increasing "diversity," or the representation of "underrepresented" groups.

So, ironically, by improving the economic status of white, two-earner families through improved opportunities for white women, affirmative action ended up benefiting the very white males who most fiercely resisted it. Although affirmative action was conceived as a tool to "make the playing fields equal," economic progress for blacks and other minorities continued to be hindered by substantial disparities in income, wealth, status, and employment as well as higher rates of poverty (Darity & Myers, 1998; Oliver & Shapiro, 1995).

Race, Equity and Higher Education

The counterpoint to the concentration of wealth is the concentration of poverty. As the good times rolled for white couples and white families, black couples and black families withered under the grinding stones of poverty and deprivation (Wilson, 1996). In fact, the number of black children born into poverty actually increased from 43 percent in 1968 to 45 percent in 1998 (U.S. Department of Housing and Urban Development, 1999). In 1996, 22.2 percent of African Americans were not covered by any form of health insurance compared to only 12 percent of whites (U.S. Census Bureau, 1996). The chronically poor economic status of Blacks has direct consequences for educational attainment, affecting early schooling opportunities, test performance, grades and funding for college (Darity & Myers, 1998; Farley & Allen, 1987).

This is the history that brings us to the present, a moment where American higher education is in a process of resegregation. For African Americans in particular, low rates of college enrollment and degree attainment had caused concern. Since the rollback of affirmative action in 1995, black and Latino and Latina enrollments at the University of California's most prestigious campuses, Berkeley, and Los Angeles, have dropped by roughly 50 percent. At these institutions, the gains for blacks in college enrollment and earned degrees are now being reversed. More generally, since the early 1960s, African Americans had made significant gains in enrollment and degree attainment at the university level. The percentage of African Americans who completed four years of college or more rose from 4 percent in 1962 to 15.5 percent in 1999 (U.S. Census Bureau, 2000). However, the representation of African Americans in this category compared to other racial groups remains relatively poor. Although undergraduate enrollment for African Americans increased 8.3 percent since 1993, the rise is less than half the rates of increase for Chicano/Latino, Asian Americans, and Native Americans during the same period (Wilds, 2000).

Compared to their white counterparts, black disparities in enrollment are even more alarming. Most recent data show that African Americans comprise less than 12 percent of the total undergraduate enrollment nationally, whereas whites make up 71 percent of the student population. Moreover, among bachelor's degrees awarded in 1997, African Americans received only 8.1 percent, though they represented more than 11.2 percent of all undergraduate students (Wilds, 2000). At the same time, whites were awarded 77 percent of bachelor's degrees with 71 percent undergraduate enrollment. If the disproportionate contributions of Historically Black Colleges and Universities to total Black student enrollment and earned degrees were removed, these figures would be even more lopsided.

College enrollment rates and participation in higher education for Chicanos/Latinos are often comparable in relationship to African Americans. Since 1974, the percentage of both Latinos and Latinas who completed four years of college or more rose from 5.5 percent in 1974 to 11 percent in 1999 (U.S. Census Bureau, 2000). Moreover, Chicano/Latino total enrollment in higher education increased 79.2 percent from 1988 to 1997 (Wilds, 2000), the highest gain of the four major racial groups. Although Chicanos/Latinos have a 45-percent completion rate at Division I colleges and their enrollment rates have increased 8 percentage points since 1990, they continue to trail both whites and African Americans in obtaining four-year degrees. Although Chicanos/Latinos represent 9 percent of undergraduate students, they were awarded only 5.3 percent of all bachelor's degrees in 1997 (Wilds, 2000).

On the other hand, Asian Americans made significant gains in enrollment, degree attainment and participation in higher education over the period. Their enrollment in higher education increased 73 percent from 1988 to 1997 and they were awarded 6 percent of all bachelor's degrees in 1997 (Wilds, 2000).

In California, the effects of anti-affirmative action legislation have directly impeded the participation and degree attainment of blacks and Latinos in the University of California system. For example, while in 1997 nearly 50 blacks and 50 Chicanos/Latinos enrolled in the UCLA Law School, the class of this year's entering class numbered only 2 black students and 17 Chicanos/Latinos.

This is the nature of the crisis involving race, equity and affirmative action in U.S. higher education. We see a return to apartheid higher educational systems that either completely excluded or allowed a few token blacks (and Chicanos/Latinos).

Pointedly, much of the move to segregate American higher education has come under the guise of improving academic standards and academic quality. Blacks are implicitly and explicitly identified as "threats" to academic quality; where their numbers grow, it is taken as evidence of lowered academic standards. Thus, this line of reasoning implicitly asserts, the best way to improve academic reputation is to exclude blacks or greatly limit their presence.

The state of California provides much of the impetus for the anti-affirmative action movement, largely as a result of poor educational policy and planning. Over the past three decades, the state's population nearly doubled (Table 1).

Table 1: California Population, 1960-1990

YEAR	RACE					
	ASIAN	BLACK	HISPANIC	NATIVE AMERICAN	WHITE	TOTAL
1960	--	--	--	--	--	15,717,204
1970	671,210	1,379,537	2,423,610	83,787	15,480,856	20,039,000
1980	1,257,408	1,794,051	4,615,711	164,710	15,950,120	23,782,000
1990	2,746,186	2,105,283	7,775,263	185,126	17,132,143	29,944,000
1998	3,724,845	2,357,377	9,938,776	197,521	17,275,835	33,494,354

Source: California Department of Finance, Demographic Research Unit

From 1970 to 1998, California's black population grew by 71 percent, an impressive rate of population growth under most circumstances. However, this rapid growth was virtually insignificant alongside the astounding rates of increase for California's Chicano/Latino and Asian-American populations. From 1970 to 1998, the state's Latino population grew by over 450 percent (to 9.9 million, from 2.4 million) while the Asian-American population grew by over 500 percent (671,210 to 3,724,845) (California Department of Finance, 1999).

California's political leaders didn't anticipate the consequences of this population boom for the state's higher education system, thus contributing to severe demand/supply discrepancies in higher education. Instead of adding beds in college dorms, these administrations invested in exponential increases in the number of prison beds—an investment decision that made neither sound fiscal nor moral sense. Since 1984, there have been twenty-one prisons built in California, but only three state university campuses and no University of California campus—despite the fact that incarcerating someone annually costs the state more than ten times as much as a student's standard in-state tuition ($25,000 vs. $2,250) (Bureau of Justice Statistics, 2000).

What Future for Affirmative Action in American Higher Education?

Will the educational future for America's colleges and universities be racial re-segregation, or will the students these institutions enroll in *look like America looks* in all its rich, racial, ethnic and cultural diversity? Vigorous struggles are being waged across the U.S. as a national conservative coalition, led by organizations such as the Center for Individual Rights in Washington, DC, mount a series of court cases intended to overturn the operation of affirmative action programs at all levels of the educational pipeline. Suits have been brought recently, or are pending, against: a UCLA operated early childhood/elementary school; against elementary schools for high-achievers in Boston and San Francisco; against undergraduate admissions programs at the Universities of Michigan and Georgia; against a financial aid program for high-achieving African Americans at the University of Maryland; as well as against Law Schools at the Universities of Michigan and Texas. In addition, the anti-affirmative action movement has sought, with some success, to pass state laws banning the operation of affirmative action programs that take race into account in college admissions decisions, and, relying on conservative judges, to secure judicial decisions narrowing permissible actions by public institutions to remedy past and current discrimination

But it is important to note that progressive forces have not conceded defeat. In fact, there is a strong and growing counter national movement to defend affirmative action and to resist the re-segregation of American higher education. It includes students across the country who are organizing and demonstrating in defense of affirmative action under the banner of The Coalition to Defend Affirmative Action By Any Means Necessary (BAMN), which was founded in July 1995 at the University of California at Berkeley. BAMN has actively supported not only the defense of affirmative action in California but also at the University of Michigan Law School and its undergraduate college.

In addition, the NAACP Legal Defense Fund, the Mexican American Legal Defense Fund, the Asian Pacific American Legal Center and the American Civil Liberties Union have sought to protect affirmative action. In some cases, they have filed *amici* briefs to support universities that are being charged with "reverse discrimination" against white students, and, in other instances, filed suits on behalf of students of color who were denied educational opportunities because of racially discriminatory admissions processes or inferior resources, curricula or facilities in the public, secondary school systems.

Progressive scholars have begun to produce significant research that refutes the notion that American society is "colorblind," and thus there is no longer any need for the continued operation of affirmative action programs. *The Shape of the River: Long-Term Consequences of Considering Race in College and University Admissions,* by William G.

Bowen, and Derek Bok, systematically documents the social benefits of affirmative action in higher education for the larger society. Their book also destroys claims about the academic calibre and performance of black students admitted to prestigious colleges and universities under affirmative action; their research shows that these students achieve academically, and that a high percentage graduate and disproportionately go on to careers in public service. In a similar vein, proceedings from a Stanford University-sponsored conference organized by Kenji Hakuta, James Jones and Mitchell Chang, titled "Facing the Courts of Law and Public Opinion: Social Science Evidence on Diversity in Higher Education," documented the positive educational benefits of diversity for teaching and learning in colleges and universities. The conference proceedings concluded that affirmative action in higher education continued to be warranted and provided extensive, positive benefits for the larger society.

Developments such as these bode well for the continuation of affirmative action in higher education. The political stance of the University of California Board of Regents has shifted enough to provoke a discussion of overturning the previous Board's ban of affirmative action in University hiring and contracting. Even more encouraging is the gathering political movement to hold another statewide referendum on whether to reverse Proposition 209 (passed in 1995), which banned the consideration of race in college admissions.

What Future for Race, Economics and Educational Opportunity?

America continues to wrestle with the issue of whether race and ethnicity will be the ground for unity or division. Nowhere is this sobering assessment so vividly portrayed than in California. In California, 39 percent of African-American men in their twenties are in prison, on probation or paroled (Bureau of Justice Statistics, 2000). At the same time, blacks, Chicanos/Latinos, and Native Americans (and yes, even Asian Americans) are woefully underrepresented in college attendance and among those in positions of esteem and power. Between 1989 and 1998, while California's African-American population has remained consistent, the University of California system has experienced an 18.1 percent decrease in the number of African Americans (See Table 2 on page 98).

The economic situation is often the trigger for these contests—certainly, this has been the case in California.

When California experienced economic downturns due to layoffs in the space industry and other manufacturing sectors, the state's social fabric was severely strained: people panicked, resorting to stereotyping, racial hostility, economic exclusion, xenophobia and discriminatory politics. Predictably the psychological and real burden from this "lashing out" fell disproportionately on African Americans, Chicanos/Latinos and immigrants; but especially on blacks.

In this sense, California is a metaphor for the status of race in America during these, the dawning moments of the twenty-first century. What is valuable about the California case is the state's ability to place in stark relief the complex intricacy of the nation's race problems in the new century. Racial conflict is shown to be bound in race-ethnic conflict *and* in conflict based on national origin.

The emphasis in America on domination—and its companion, degradation—wreaks profound human and societal havoc. The paradigm of white supremacy, domination and exclusion cuts across the areas of education, health, politics, criminal justice and the economy (Morris, Allen, Maurrasse, & Gilbert, 1995). Affirmative action inclusiveness and diversity have the power to enrich the higher education experience for all involved (Hurtado, Milem, Clayton-Pedersen, & Allen, 1999). Ultimately exploitative violence weakens not only those outside the mainstream or in the shadows, but the society at large. The choices are really quite simple: will the country opt to live up to the inspirational American Creed, offering freedom, opportunity and equality to all, or will it continue to deny these ideals and by so doing lay the foundation for the destruction of yet another great civilization?

Table 2: Undergraduate Enrollment by Ethnicity at the University of California, 1989 to 1998

Fall Term	Total Students	Asian/ Pacific Islander	Black	Filipino	Latino	Native American	Other	White	Total, Declared Ethnicity	Non-Resident Alien	No Response
1989	123,441	22,993	5,796	4,102	13,071	1,121	1,609	68,187	116,879	2,554	4,008
1990	124,271	25,093	5,622	4,270	14,191	1,206	1,565	65,549	117,496	2,306	4,469
1991	124,627	27,224	5,327	4,334	14,778	1,301	1,504	62,602	117,070	2,443	5,114
1992	124,226	29,265	5,053	4,414	15,204	1,248	1,628	59,337	116,149	2,373	5,704
1993	122,271	31,642	4,911	4,469	15,395	1,194	1,710	54,840	114,161	2,317	5,793
1994	121,615	34,194	4,848	4,626	16,096	1,173	1,824	51,324	114,085	2,420	5,110
1995	123,737	36,327	5,009	4,982	16,956	1,234	2,024	49,804	116,336	2,569	4,832
1996	126,048	37,949	4,965	5,290	17,228	1,229	2,201	49,531	118,393	2,632	5,023
1997	128,689	39,257	4,988	5,644	17,131	1,195	2,482	50,240	120,937	2,800	4,952
1998	132,189	39,813	4,749	5,962	16,905	1,149	2,588	49,879	121,045	2,726	8,418
Percent Change	7.1%	73.2%	-18.1%	45.3%	29.3%	2.5%	60.8%	-26.8%	3.6%	6.7%	110.0%

Souce: California Postsecondary Education Commission, Student Profiles, 1999

References

Allen, Walter R., and Joseph O. Jewell. 1995. African-American education since *An American dilemma*: An American dilemma revisited. *Daedalus, 124*(1), 77-100.

Bowen, William G., and Derek Bok. (1998). *The Shape of the River: Long-Term Consequences of Considering Race in College and University Admissions.* Princeton, NJ: Princeton University Press.

Bureau of Justice Statistics, 2000.

California Department of Corrections, 2000.

California Department of Finance, 1999.

Collins, Patricia Hill. 1998. *Fighting Words: Black Women and the Search for Justice.* Minneapolis, MN: University of Minnesota Press.

Darity, William, and Samuel Myers Jr. 1998. *Persistent Disparity: Race and Economic Inequality in the United States Since 1945.* Cheltenham, UK: Edward Elgar.

Farley, Reynolds, and Walter R. Allen. 1987. *The Color Line and the Qquality of Life in America.* Oxford: Oxford University Press.

Hochschild, Jennifer L. 1995. *Facing up to the American Dream: Race, Class and the Soul of the Nation.* Princeton, NJ: Princeton University Press.

Hurtado, Sylvia, Jeffrey Milem, Alma Clayton-Pedersen and Walter R. Allen. 1999. *Enacting Diverse Learning Environments: Improving the Climate for Racial/Ethnic Diversity in Higher Education.* ASHE-ERIC Higher Education Report, Volume 26, No. 8. Washington, DC: The George Washington University, Graduate School of Education and Human Development.

Johnson, Lyndon B. 1965, June 4. To fulfill these rights. Commencement Address, Howard University, Washington, DC.

Morris, Aldon, Walter R. Allen, David Maurrasse, and Derrick Gilbert. 1995. "White supremacy and higher education: The Alabama higher education desegregation case." *National Black Law Journal, 14*(1), 59-91.

Oliver, Melvin L., and Thomas M. Shapiro. 1995. *Black Wealth/White Wealth: A New Perspective on Racial Inequality.* New York: Routledge.

Report of the National Advisory Commission on Civil Disorders. 1968. Introduction by Tom Wicker. New York: Bantam Books.

U.S. Census Bureau, 1996.

U.S. Department of Housing and Urban Development, 1999.

U.S. Department of Justice, 2000.

U.S. Bureau of the Census. 2000. *Population Profile of the United States: 1997.* Washington, DC: U.S. Government Printing Office.

Wilds, D.J. 2000. *Minorities in Higher Education 1999-2000: Seventeenth Annual Status Report.* Washington, DC: American Council on Education.

Wilson, H. 1998. "Does affirmative action for Blacks harm Whites? Some evidence from the higher education arena." *Western Journal of Black Studies*, *22*(4), 218.

Wilson, William Julius. 1996. *When Work Disappears: The World of the New Urban Poor.* New York: Alfred A. Knopf.

School Choice: The Option of Success

BY DEIRDRE BAILEY

"There comes a time when the cup of endurance runs over and men are no longer willing to be plunged into the abyss of despair."

In his powerful "Letter from a Birmingham Jail," Martin Luther King, Jr. offered the quotation above as part of a poignant response to a group of Alabama clergymen who criticized non-violent, direct action as an inappropriate and untimely mechanism of challenging the evils of Southern segregation. Today, almost forty years later, a similar lack of tolerance is being proclaimed by a segment of the black community refusing to accept another decade of failing urban public schools. No longer is it enough to champion urban education reform movements, which author Diane Ravitch warns should be "avoided like the plague." In her latest book, *Left Back: A Century of Failed School Reforms*, a history of public education and its numerous reforms since the turn of the century, she demonstrates that the traditional system has not lived up to its promise of a quality education for all Americans.

Throughout the country—in rural and urban areas—black children are trapped in schools that provide a sub-par education and place low expectations on their academic achievement. Most of these children and their families do not possess the financial capabilities to move to a better school district or pay for tuition at private or parochial schools. Instead, their only hope is to ignite genuine change by giving parents the freedom to choose the best educational environment for their children. Such "in-the-meantime" strategies—vouchers, public and private run charters and tuition scholarships, among others—are thought to provide poor parents with immediate alternatives while the traditional public system attempts to reform itself. In the late 1960s, psychologist Kenneth B. Clark, who helped write the NAACP court brief for the *Brown* school desegregation case in 1954, went so far as to suggest in an article in the Harvard Educational Review that, "[P]ublic education need not be identified with the present system ... of public schools. [It] can be more broadly and pragmatically defined in terms of ... an educational system which is in the public interest." Proponents of school choice would contend Clark's words support their own assertions that alternative forms of public education are needed to fulfill America's promise of a democratic education for all children and ensure their constructive participation in society. They contend that it's unrealistic to expect any significant improvement in performance from troubled school systems, as long as they remain assured of increasing state aid, federal aid and a steady supply of students. However, it is also naïve to assume that aggressive competition for both students and public dollars alone can solve the pervasive problem of low academic performance in troubled public schools. The wiser course is to support simultaneous attempts—through both systemic reform and outside competition—to strengthen our present system of public education as part of an overall strategy to improve the educational destiny of the majority of black children.

School Choice and the Black Community

Evidence that school choice is gaining momentum in the black community can be found in the 1999 edition of the Joint Center for

Political and Economic Studies Opinion Poll. Sixty percent of black respondents indicated support for school vouchers, an increase of 25 percent from the previous year's survey. Not surprisingly, a majority of black respondents reported that their public schools have gotten worse over the past five years.

In its *Achievement in America* 2000 publication, the Education Trust, Inc. provides validation to the growing sense that urban schools are not working. The report suggests that twelfth graders in high poverty areas read at the same level as eighth graders in affluent areas. Similarly, the report includes figures from the U.S. Department of Education, which reveal that an "A" in high poverty areas is equivalent to a "C" in affluent areas.

The emergence of a well-organized black group, promoting controversial alternatives, such as vouchers and for-profit school management, also affirms the idea that the black community is growing impatient with the current system of public education. The Black Alliance for Educational Options (BAEO), a newly established national organization, is designed to ensure that black children have the greatest opportunities for academic success by actively supporting parental choice and educating parents about the various educational options available for their children. Since its formation in 2000, BAEO has organized almost twenty chapters in major cities throughout the United States. The organization's leader is Howard Fuller, former superintendent of Milwaukee public schools, who resigned in 1995 after an anti-school choice teachers' union gained control of the elected school board.

Former New York Congressman Floyd Flake, Ohio Secretary of State Kenneth Blackwell and Pennsylvania State Representative Dwight Evans are among BAEO's national board of directors. The organization has spent most of its first year spreading its message about the benefits of educational options to the black community. Its most important organizing event, the Symposium on Educational Options for African Americans, attracted over 700 participants from across the country to Milwaukee in March of 2001. Attempting to spread its message even further, BAEO has launched a multi-million dollar national advertisement campaign on major television networks and in newspapers in several targeted cities. School choice for BAEO does not rest with vouchers alone. The organization also supports public school initiatives such as charter and magnet schools.

School Choice and the Black Establishment

On the other hand, the black establishment of Democratic elected officials and organizational leaders continue to support the traditional public school system despite increasing criticism of its inadequate results among poor minority children. Members of the Congressional Black Caucus (CBC) and leaders of organizations such as the National Association for the Advancement of Colored People (NAACP) and the National Alliance of Black School Educators (NABSE) remain opposed to any form of school choice that takes the responsibility for educating black children out of the control of the public bureaucracy. Only recently have charter schools been embraced in a limited form by many black organizations.

Some observers have said that the black establishment is threatened by any system that directly challenges the institution in which a segment of the black middle class has flourished and teacher unions have garnered political strength. Much of the opposition voiced by black leaders is driven by suspicions that conservatives are using the African-American community as a ploy to gain greater school choice for their more affluent constituencies. In the February issue of *Black Enterprise*, Congressman Harold Ford, Jr. charged that the "real beneficiaries of any voucher program are middle and upper-middle income families, although the rhetoric is primarily aimed at what [Republicans] call under-performing schools." Despite those comments, the publicly-supported voucher programs that exist—there are just three in the country: Cleveland, Florida, and Milwaukee—are restricted to either families whose incomes fall below the national poverty rate or whose children attend low-performing schools. Both the Milwaukee Parental Choice Program (MPCP) and the Cleveland Scholarship and Tutoring Program (CSTP) are specifically designed to serve low-income families. For instance, in Milwaukee, families participating in the MPCP must have incomes at or below 175 percent of the federal poverty level of ($30,043 for a family of four in 2000). Similarly, in Cleveland priority is given to families based on the federal poverty level ($17,050 for a family of four in 2000). On the other hand, the Florida A+ Opportunity Scholarship Program (FA+OSP) places its emphasis on students who attend public schools that have been designated by the Florida Department of Education as "failing" for two out of four years—a label that frequently correlates with the family income of a school's student population.

In a widely-noted comment, Reverend Eugene Rivers, the Boston community activist, suggests that "most black politicians and other elites are not accountable to a poor black base." Rivers' remarks beg the question of why the black establishment staunchly opposes a system that would give black children a chance to receive a better education. The answer appears to be entwined in a difference of opinion about what the best approach is for ensuring that black children in failing schools gain exposure to what Harvard professor Ronald Ferguson calls an "instructional regime," an approach that is attentive to the needs of individual children and puts no ceiling on student progress. For a growing portion of the black community, such a level of accountability can only be accomplished by infusing effective competition into the present system. The black establishment, along with other liberal advocates of the traditional public system, prefers that resources be used to replicate the techniques that account for private school success—a model that has posted significant results in many urban areas throughout the country.

Five Policy Implications to School Choice

Money Following the Child. In order to move to a comprehensive system of school choice, the way public education is funded would require total reconstruction. A policy model that moves the current public system from a placed-based funding scheme in which state funding is directly appropriated to a local school district to a structure that transfers the state per-pupil allocation directly to the parent's school of choice—whether public, parochial or private—would need to be carefully designed and implemented.

Increasing Educational Options for Low-income Parents. The dialogue surrounding school choice in the black community must focus on how to provide quality and financially affordable educational options to poor families. Efforts should be concentrated at the state and local levels of government to pass legislation that authorizes school choice programs for poor children in failing schools—providing complete tuition assistance and safeguards against potentially discriminatory entrance procedures at private schools. The Milwaukee Parental Choice Program provides a useful model.

Conceptually Redefining What Public Education Means. Dr. Kenneth Clark offers a definition of public education that moves beyond the traditional public system and focuses more on developing a system that is in the public interest. A public interest approach to education would reject any system, whether public or private, that failed to properly educate children and would more aptly concentrate on ensuring that whomever delivered educational services was held accountable for the academic performance of students in the public system.

Challenges to Reaching the Masses of Underserved Children. The school choice movement will increasingly face the challenge of how to impact the majority of black and Latino children that attend failing public schools. Two approaches—if equally embraced—might help cast a larger net around our children:

- Support infusing viable, effective competition into the traditional public system to increase accountability and encourage improvement.
- Genuinely commit to a dual effort to expand educational options *and* improve urban public schools.

Fiscal Considerations of Providing More Educational Options. Opponents of school choice programs argue that charter schools and publicly supported tuition-based schools drain the school district of much needed and relied upon dollars. However, part of the goal of expanding educational options for poor children is to create an atmosphere of competition that forces public schools to improve or face extinction to more preferred schools. To achieve a harmonious atmosphere in which school choice advocates and public school administrators work collectively to improve public education, efforts to secure separate government funding for vouchers and charter schools, could be sought in a joint lobbying effort by both parties.

A School Model that Works

In the South Bronx, one of the most economically distressed areas in New York, a recently converted charter school is making tremendous gains toward improving academic achievement among poor black and Latino children. KIPP Academy (an acronym for Knowledge is Power Program) is one of four "sub-schools" and the only conversion school located in Intermediate School 151. It has roughly 250 students, 93 percent of who qualify for federal breakfast and lunch programs. The two KIPP Academies—one in New York, the other in Houston—were conceived almost six years ago by David Levin and Michael Feinberg, both former Teach for America corps members and graduates of Yale University and the University of Pennsylvania, respectively.

Levin, who is currently principal of KIPP-New York, admits

spending most days responding to criticisms of being a white man helping black children. "I build bridges," says Levin, "a body of work to be judged by that allows me to build bridges." KIPP-New York is made up entirely of black and Latino students. Levin, who is Jewish, says he is driven by the ideas of black scholars, such as historian Carter G. Woodson whom he frequently cites. "The education system is designed to oppress minority children," asserts Levin "but if implemented correctly, it can be used to liberate."

Levin and Feinberg learned this first-hand as protégés of Harriett Ball, an African-American teacher, during their tenure as Teach for America recruits in Houston. She taught 4th grade at Bastin Elementary School where Levin assumed his first teaching assignment. Both founders credit Ball with helping them become better teachers. "I didn't know how to teach," says Levin. "Once, she came into my classroom and taught my students in 45 minutes what I had been trying to teach them for three weeks."

A teaching method developed by Ball to get at-risk students excited about learning is Rap, Rhythm & Rhyme. Ball's techniques incorporate chanting and clapping into math and language instruction. In fact, the name KIPP derives from one of Ball's signature chants, "The more I read, the more I know/The more I know, the more I grow/The more I talk, the less I know/Because knowledge is power/Power is money/And I want it!/You've got to read, baby, read!"

I recently went to New York to observe KIPP in action and became convinced that academic excellence is an attainable goal among underprivileged minority students. One of the best ways to accomplish this is to learn from successful schools that actually change the fate of urban youngsters through high academic standards and fearless commitment. I offer KIPP-New York (henceforth "KIPP") and its five pillars as a model. There are hundreds of other schools throughout the country making a difference in the lives of our children.

A Statistical Analysis of KIPP's Success 1999-2000
(Based on New York State's revised scoring system)

CTB Reading Scores	1998-1999 (Percent of students performing at or above grade-level)	1999-2000 (Percent of students performing at or above grade-level)	One-year Improvement
Grade 5	30% (pre-KIPP)	58%	+93%
Grade 6	52%	61%	+15%
Grade 7	54%	70%	+29%
KIPP Total Grade 5-7	47%	63%	+34%
District 7	20%	25%	+25%
New York City	36%	41%	+14%

KIPP Grade 8 New York State ELA Exam	44%	55%	+25%
District 7	17%	16%	-6%
New York City	35%	33%	-6%

CTB Math Scores	1998-1999 (Percent of students performing at or above grade-level)	1999-2000 (Percent of students performing at or above grade-level)	One-year Improvement
Grade 5	43% (pre-KIPP)	71%	+65%
Grade 6	32%	32%	+0%
Grade 7	47%	63%	+34%
KIPP Total Grade 5-7	41%	55%	+34%
District 7	17%	17%	+0%
New York City	34%	34%	+0%

KIPP Grade 8 New York State ELA Exam	58%	66%	+14%
District 7	8%	9%	+13%
New York City	23%	23%	+0%

KIPP Student Daily Attendance = 96%
(Including all hours 7:25 a.m. - 5:00 p.m., Saturdays, and summer school)

High Expectations

KIPP is a "tough love," no-nonsense kind of place. A set of high standards and sacrifice is instilled in its students from the time most of them enter at the fifth grade to their graduation at eighth grade. The school's motto, "There Are No Short Cuts" and other slogans, such as "Team Always Beats Individual" are posted throughout the school as constant reminders that hard work and commitment are essential ingredients of academic success. KIPP students are routinely reminded that their attitudes have an effect on their aptitude. "Be Nice!! Work Hard!!" is also a familiar slogan adorning school walls.

All of KIPP's eight graders complete a two-year, high school level Algebra I course by the time they graduate. During my visit, I received an informal lesson from an eighth grade student who was capable of explaining what an idiom meant in its literal and figurative form. Equally impressive was a sixth grade reading class where two students eagerly raised their hands to share with the class an "inference" and then, a "prediction" regarding the book, *The Giver* by Lois Lowry.

More Time

At KIPP, the school day promptly begins at 7:25 a.m. with an hour of critical thinking instruction. Students interested in participating in the school's breakfast program must arrive by 7 a.m. Only after nine and one-half hours does the official school day end at 5 p.m., when after-school tutorials begin. Simply put: KIPP invests 67 percent more instructional time in its students than the national average.

More time—in the form of a longer school day, Saturday school and an extended school year—is intentionally used to catch students up academically and to work on developing strong character traits, such as respect, discipline and kindness, that will help them go farther in life. The longer KIPP has its students, the less likely they are to be influenced by the crime, drugs and gangs that saturate their neighborhood.

Focus on Results

Part of the longer school day is also focused on preparing students for standardized tests without interfering with core subject matter instruction. During the 1998-99 school year, only a third of KIPP's newly admitted fifth graders performed at or above grade level on the New York State reading exam. However, in the following school year, close to 60 percent of these same students performed at grade level or higher. Such tremendous improvements, has earned KIPP the honor of being the highest performing public middle school in the Bronx in reading and math for three straight years. High test scores, for many KIPP students, will be the only things that save them from being stigmatized and denied equal access to college and career opportunities.

This year, more than 90 percent of KIPP's graduates will begin high school at prestigious private, parochial and boarding schools throughout the country—Loomis Chaffee, Phillips Andover and Choate Rosemary Hall, to name a few. Not every KIPP student has the necessary test scores to automatically qualify for admissions, but because of their mastery of a rigorous middle-school curriculum, many schools take a chance and offer them scholarships to attend. KIPP views non-public schools as the best high school environment for its alumni. "Most students who do well in public schools are able to function independently," says Levin, "our students still need the structure that is found in private schools."

Choice and Commitment

The attrition rate among KIPP students is relatively low, two to three percent a year, mostly due to family relocation and an occasional departure by a family refusing to submit to KIPP's philosophy. It's not a zoned school, which means parents choose to send their children, if fortunate enough to have a slot open up. KIPP's 96 percent daily student attendance rate suggests that both parents and students are satisfied with their school choice.

Teachers, students and parents sign contracts that govern their roles as active contributors to the students' success. A similar pledge in everyone's contract promises to always be available to members of the school community and any concerns they might have. For teachers, this often means making themselves accessible after school hours—as did a teacher I observed closing out class by urging students to call him later if questions should arise about that evening's math homework.

Power to Lead

As a charter school, KIPP administrators have authority to make budgetary and personnel decisions free of the district's bureaucracy. Decisions regarding what curricula approach to use and when the time comes for an ineffective teacher to be dismissed are all made on-site. KIPP is also able to do a significant amount of fundraising to supplement the per-pupil budget that it receives from the district. Most of these additional funds go toward compensating teachers for working longer hours and most recently, to help pay private school tuition for KIPP graduates.

The autonomy that KIPP enjoys actually preceded its conversion to a charter school this year. It was founded under a special agreement with the Bronx school district that gave KIPP privileges not granted to most public schools. Levin agreed to take the district's lowest performing middle-school students and turn them into high achievers in exchange for the space and freedom to do so.

Conclusion

If increasing the life chances of black youngsters through a strong system of public education is our goal, then the black community and the black establishment must quickly come together to reconcile their differences and devise a plan to help black students. Partisan politics and ideological disagreements must stop at the steps of our schools to ensure that the greatest efforts are made on behalf of our neediest children.

We cannot afford to lose the promise and sanctity that our schools are supposed to represent, especially considering the plethora of social ills that plague urban communities. Charles Highsmith, principal of Strawberry Mansion High School in Philadelphia, provides us a valuable compass: "Our special victories come when we don't let them fail—no matter what personal challenges of poverty, family crises, or neighborhood blight confront them."

References

Black Alliance for Educational Options (BAEO). *www.baeoonline.org*.

Clark, Kenneth B. 1968. "Alternative Public School System." Harvard Educational Review, Winter.

The Education Trust, Inc. 2000. "Achievement in America 2000." *www.edtrust.org*, Washington, DC.

Ferguson, Ronald F. 1998. Can Schools Narrow the Black-White Test Score Gap, *The Black-White Test Score Gap*, The Brookings Institute.

Fuller, Howard L. "The Continuing Struggle of African Americans for the Power to Make Real Educational Choices." Second Annual Symposium on Educational Options for African Americans, March 2-5, 2000.

Fuller, Howard L. March 2-5, 2000. *The Saturation of Lies and Distortions About Educational Vouchers*, Second Annual Symposium on Educational Options for African Americans.

Highsmith, Charles. March 18, 2001. "Setting Goals and Following Through." *The Philadelphia Inquirer.*

Hill, David. January 17, 2001. Rap, Rhythm, and Rhyme. Education Week.

Interview with Kaleem Caire, Executive Director of BAEO. April 2001.

Interview with David Levin, Principal of KIPP Academy (New York). March 2001.

Joint Center for Political and Economic Studies, 1999. 1999 National Opinion Poll—Education. Washington, DC.

Joseph, Gar. March 17, 1998. "Analyst Has Good Marx, *The Philadelphia Daily News.*

Joyce Jones. February 2000. "Why the CBC Opposes School Vouchers," *Black Enterprise.*

King, Jr. Martin L. 1963. Letter from a Birmingham Jail.

Knowledge Is Power Program (KIPP), *www.kipp.org.*

Knowledge Is Power Program (KIPP). 2000. "Highlights of the KIPP Academy."

Knowledge Is Power Program (KIPP). 1999-2000. "A Statistical Analysis of KIPP's Success."

Knowledge Is Power Program (KIPP). 2000. "KIPP Commitment to Excellence Form."

The National Alliance of Black School Educators (NABSE), *www.nabse.org.*

Niebuhr, Gustav. April 7, 2001. *A Point Man for the Bush Church-State Collaboration, The New York Times.*

Price, Hugh B. December 13, 1999. *The ABCs of Urban School Reform,* To Be Equal.

Raspberry, William. August 21, 2000. "Cold-Shouldering Success," *The Washington Post.*

Ravitch, Diane. 2000. *Left Back: A Century of Failed School Reforms,* New York: Simon & Schuster.

School Choice Info.org, *www.schoolchoiceinfo.org.*

Black Homeownership: Housing and Black Americans Under 35

BY ANGELA D. JAMES

Ask any American to define the "American Dream" and you'd be hard pressed to find a single person who would do so without mentioning homeownership. The dream of owning a home of one's own is pervasive for practical, financial and cultural reasons. Thus, it's no wonder that after several generations of rising rates of income, education, and homeownership among Americans, there's growing concern that the current generation of young adults face a more difficult transition to adulthood status and all its rewards than their predecessors. Middle class stauts, as exemplified by homeownership, appears to be more difficult for the current generation to attain. The generation of Americans who entered the labor market during the 1980s and 1990s, often referred to as "generation X," are the first to face the prospect of having a lower standard of living than their parents (Newman, 1993; Farley, 2000). Blacks, who tend to share the economic and social trends of the larger populace, have been hit particularly hard by the adverse economic trends of the last several decades (Wilson, 1988; Tucker & Mitchell Kernan, 1995). While white Generation X'ers may be having a more difficult time acquiring the home of their all-American dreams, for black Generation X'ers, this dream is far more likely to remain just that, a dream.

If it does, the inability to secure what has always been a critical symbol of middle-class status—and a foundation for accumulating assets—could profoundly undermine their, and all of Black America's, quest for full inclusion into American society. Generation X'ers are the demographic cohort that has historically been a common point of entry for individuals into homeownership. Thus, the importance of being able to buy a home at this age, in terms of individuals accumulating family assets, and in terms of establishing a standard of living and an overall sense of well being, can't be overstated. If a substantial proportion of the current cohort of African-American Generation X'ers are unable to become homeowners, then the prospects of significantly reducing the wealth gap between blacks and whites in the future are likely to be bleak.

Historical Overview of Homeownership in the United States

The image of the suburban homeowner is a powerful part of the image of the middle-class American; few phenomena exemplify aspirations of the American middle class as powerfully (Gans, 1988; Horton, 1992; Farley, 2000). Surveys of housing preferences as well as analyses of housing behavior suggest that homeownership continues to be a major life goal of most Americans.

The reasons for this preference aren't hard to imagine. For one thing, the financial benefits of homeownership are substantial. Homeowners are accorded many important tax advantages: To name just two, housing expenses can be deducted from income before taxation, which substantially reduces the financial impact of expenditures (Myers, 1995); and homeowners, unlike renters, are able to build equity as they simply go about the business of financing "the roof over their head." Equity from one's home can be used to guarantee other economic ventures, to finance the college education of one's children, or to support retirement. In this way, homeownership represents not only an integral part of the American Dream, but also the primary means of wealth accumulation in this country.

Homeowners enjoy many non-economic advantages as well. Rental units are typically not as large and do not offer as much private outdoor space as do owner-occupied units (Myers, 1995). Homeowners generally have more freedom to convert physical aspects of their home to their tastes than is the case for people who are renting. Areas of the city where there are higher proportions of homeowners typically have better social services and are more stable. Yet, despite the rewards of homeownership, and the significance of homeownership as a symbol of inclusion in American culture, homeownership remains illusive for many segments of the population. Race and class continue to be central aspects of social stratification in the United States. The prism of social inequality highlighted by differences in rates of homeownership, reflect these broader parameters of social stratification.

For most of the twentieth century, less than half of all American households were homeowners. Between 1890 and 1940 the homeownership rate fluctuated right around 45 percent. Homeownership declined during the Great Depression to less than 44 percent of households. However, homeownership dramatically increased after World War II as a result of such programs as the Federal Housing Administration and Veterans Administration guaranteed loan plans. Accordingly, homeownership rates rose rapidly to 1960. The rate of increase then slowed, before substantially declining in the 1980s for the first time in more than 50 years. Between 1994 and 2000, homeownership rates began to rise again and the latest available data indicate that over 66.5 percent of all American households are owner-occupied (Office of Policy Development and Research, 2000).

Young householders, those under 35 years of age, have had particularly low rates of homeownership in recent years. The data show that 41.2 percent of Americans under the age of 35 owned their homes in 1970. Homeownership among this group increased slightly in 1980 to around 44 percent and declined sharply to 39.6 percent in 1990. (Published data on homeownership among young adults is only available from 1970-1990)

117

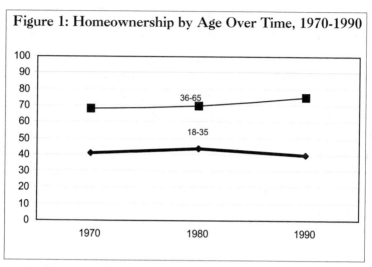

Figure 1: Homeownership by Age Over Time, 1970-1990

As figure 1 illustrates, the homeownership gap between older and younger adults has increased substantially in 1990. Homeownership among those under 35 has declined, while rates among those over 35 have increased slightly. Increasingly homeownership is polarized by age, with young cohorts facing more daunting challenges to acquiring a home.

Black households have generally had lower homeownership rates than non-Hispanic whites. Further, the gap between blacks and whites has not closed as dramatically as we might have expected in the decades since the federal Fair Housing Act and other civil rights legislation were enacted. Homeownership rates for black households increased from 35 percent in 1950 to almost 42 percent in 1970, then rose more modestly to 44 percent in 1980. This modest gain remained stagnant in decade between 1990 and the year 2000. During this period, homeownership among blacks declined by about 1 percent (Office of Policy Development and Research, 2000).

In other words, after several decades of increased opportunities for homeownership among both blacks and whites homeownership has stagnated during the last two decades. Further, as an indication of continuing racial inequality, the gap between blacks and whites has not declined significantly in the last thirty years.

A Contemporary Portrait of Homeownership: Regional and other Geographical Variation

There is considerable regional variation in rates of homeownership among blacks. Homeownership among blacks is highest in the south and lowest in the northeast. In 1990, there were only seven states where over half of black households lived in a home which they owned; six of the seven were in southern states, with the exception being Pennsylvania. While more than half of the country's black population live in central cities of metropolitan areas, homeownership rates among blacks in central cities is lower than either the rate of homeownership in suburbs or in areas outside of metropolitan areas. Nationally, only about 4 in ten black householders in the central city of metropolitan areas were homeowners, compared with about 6 in ten black householders living outside of metropolitan areas.

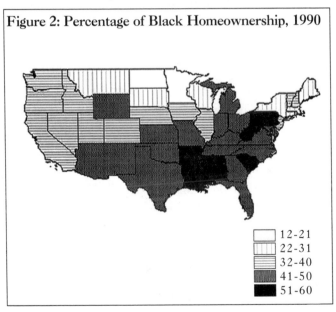

Figure 2: Percentage of Black Homeownership, 1990

12-21
22-31
32-40
41-50
51-60

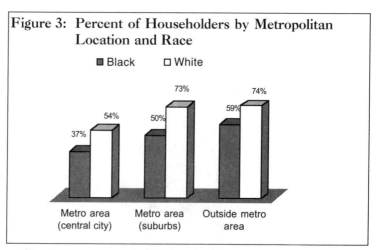

Figure 3: Percent of Householders by Metropolitan Location and Race

The gap in homeownership rates between blacks and whites is largest in the suburbs of metropolitan areas and lowest in areas outside of metropolitan areas. Significantly, there is not a single metropolitan area in the United States where blacks were as likely as whites to own their home (Bureau of Census, 1995).

Income & Education

Both income and education levels are significant predictors of homeownership. Those with higher incomes and more education are more likely to own their home than rent. The relationship between income, education and homeownership is the same for both blacks and whites. However, between those with the highest and the lowest levels of family income, the racial gap in homeownership rates persists. As figure 4 illustrates, while 90 percent of whites who earn more than $50,000 a year own their homes, only 77 percent of blacks in that income bracket do so. The racial gap at the other end of the income spectrum is even more daunting. While only 35 percent of blacks who earned less than $25,000 in family income owned their homes, about 58 percent of whites in the lowest income bracket are homeowners.

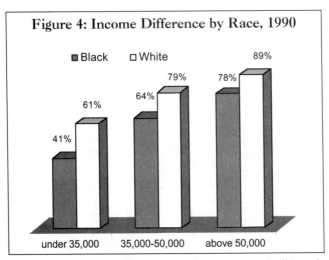

Figure 4: Income Difference by Race, 1990

Education differences in homeownership are very similar to those of income. Among blacks, those with at least a college degree are 33 percent more likely than those who do not have a high school degree to own their home. Education differences in homeownership among whites is not nearly as extreme. Eighty-one percent of white college graduates own their home, but 76 percent of whites without a high school degree have managed to convert their dream of homeownership into a reality. Consequently, while the gap in homeownership between blacks and whites with a college degrees is substantial, it is dwarfed by the 29 percentage point racial gap among those with less than a high school degree (See Figure 5).

Marital Status and Homeownership

Married people are much more likely to be homeowners than single or divorced people (Sweet, 1990). However, it remains to be seen whether the increasing diversity in family and household arrangements will fundamentally alter family-related transitions to homeownership in the future. While homeownership has increased recently among all marital status groups, married people remain much more likely than others to be homeowners. As figure 6 illustrates, there are racial gaps in home-

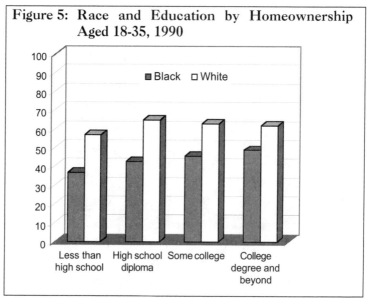

Figure 5: Race and Education by Homeownership Aged 18-35, 1990

ownership even among those most likely to own, the married. Significantly, the racial gap is greatest among young, black married couples. So, again we see that blacks under 35, in particular, face significant difficulties in attaining the American dream of homeownership and eco-

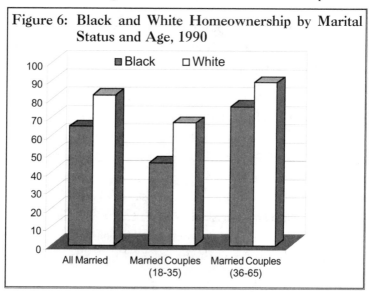

Figure 6: Black and White Homeownership by Marital Status and Age, 1990

nomic and social parity with whites.

Age Differences

The generation gap in homeownership between younger and older Americans dramatizes the growing anxieties that the former won't be able to achieve the American Dream. The inability of young people to equal, not to mention surpass, the level of social economic security of their parents became a noticeable social phenomenon in the 1980s, when homeownership became starkly polarized by age (Myers & Wolch, 1995). Homeownership prospects of the under-35 generation are hampered by a range of social factors including; stagnation in male wages, delays in marriage, historically high housing prices, and high interest rates.

The gaps between blacks and whites which exist along every social and economic marker are more dramatic when we focus on young men and women; and already pronounced racial differrences become even more evident when we examine homeownership among young adults. Among those 35 years of age and younger, only 43 percent of blacks owned their home, as opposed to a rate of 70 percent among whites in

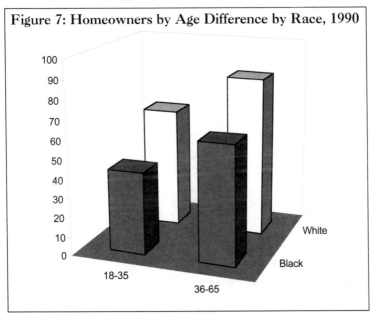

Figure 7: Homeowners by Age Difference by Race, 1990

the same age range. The struggle to enter the middle class is much greater for young African Americans, than it was for those in earlier cohorts (Myers & Wolch, 1995). In this way, macro-economic shifts causing stagnation in rates of homeownership has a wide range of social effects; higher barriers to homeownership intensify the age and racial gaps in access to opportunity.

A Multivariate Analysis of Homeownership

One question which stems from this analysis is whether racial differences between blacks and whites might be affected by their different demographic and socio-economic profiles. Higher income and education levels are associated with homeownership. Married people are more likely than the unmarried to own their home. Young adults are less likely than older adults to own their home. Might the fact that blacks are more likely to have lower education, and income, and more likely to be unmarried account for racial differences in homeownership rates? The 1980 and 1990 PUMS data, along with 2000 CPS data shows that African Americans have a much higher proportion of individuals with characteristics which decrease the likelihood of homeownership. In the first model I estimate only the effect of race on the odds of homeownership. In the second model, I estimate the importance of race, marital status, family income, education, region, race, and age on the log odds of homeownership among young adults ages 18-35. Table 1 represents the operationalization of each variable included in the model (See Table 1).

Results

The odds of homeownership is substantially lower for blacks relative to whites in each decade examined. In the first model I limit the analysis to view simply the odds of homeownership for blacks as opposed to whites. The odds of black homeownership compared to white homeownership are abysmally low. In the second model I include a range of social and demographic variables to see if the odds

Table 1: Operationalization of Variables

Variables	Measurements
Tenure	1 = Owned or being bought (loan) 0 = Rents
Race	1 = Black 0 = Non-Hispanic White
Age	Continuous
Marital Status	1 = Married, spouse present or absent 0 = Separated Divorced Widowed Never married/single
Education	0 = Less than high school diploma 1 = High school diploma 2 = Some college 3 = College degree and beyond
Region	1 = South 0 = Northwest Midwest West
Income	Continuous log odds of income
Race*Married	Interaction term between race and marital status

of black homeownership relative to whites increase to parity. Even holding constant the full range of social and demographic variables, the odds of black homeownership remains about 25 percent lower relative to whites. Further, the likelihood of homeownership among young African Americans declined substantially between 1980 and 2000. In other words, the homeownership gap between young blacks and whites, increases rather than declines over the period in question. As expected, married people have higher odds of homeownership in each decade. However, that advantage declines over time. The advantage of married over nonmarried, expressed as relative odds, are not as great in 2000, as they are in 1980. Householders living in the South also have a higher likelihood of homeownership. Those individuals with higher levels of education and income are also more likely to own their home. However, the effect of income is much stronger than that of education. Perhaps this reflects the fact that among the young, those with higher levels of education have fewer years between school leaving (and presumably a fewer number of years in the labor force) than is the case for those who stopped school with a high school degree.

The interaction term representing the interaction between race and marital status was significant in each of the decades under examination. This interaction indicates that the marriage advantage has comparatively less of an impact on the likelihood of homeownership of young African Americans. In other words, marriage does not provide the same increase in the likelihood of homeownership among blacks, as it does among whites (See Table 2, on page 129).

To revisit the initial questions fueling this investigation, it appears that:

1) controlling for other social and demographic characteristics does not eliminate the disadvantage of blacks relative to whites with regards to homeownership;

2) marital status and race interaction suggest that marriage does not faciliate homeownership for blacks in the same manner that it does for whites; and

3) the relative disadvantage to homeownership which young African Americans face has increased substantially over the course of the period between 1980 and 2000.

Conclusions

For most Americans wealth is largely centered on the ownership and value of their home. The differential rate of homeownership in the past has had a significant impact on the ability of whites and blacks, respectively, to accumulate assets and pass their wealth on to their descendants. Contemporary income and education inequality is dwarfed by racial inequality in wealth accumulation (Oliver &

Shapiro, 1995). Thus, African-American Generation X'ers have inherited an economic legacy which undermines their ability to enter the housing market. Perhaps more importantly, current declines in the rate of homeownership among young African Americans portend a future of ever greater racial inequality in the area of wealth.

Far from race disappearing when we control for the numerous social and demographic compositional differences between blacks and whites, the racial gap persists. In fact, in terms of homeownership, racial inequality has grown more severe in the last several decades. This change is particularly evident when looking at young African Americans. Young African Americans have lower odds of marriage relative to whites, and even when they marry they do not eliminate that disadvantage. The significance of this gap becomes particularly evident when controlling for income, education and other social characteristics which have been thought to drive the disadvantage of blacks relative to whites. The daunting challenge facing young African American's striving to realize the American Dream of homeownership has increased over time. Further, the value of other auxiliary social characteristics, such as marriage, in facilitating homeownership is lower for blacks than it is for whites. The research presented here suggests that racial differences cannot be explained by corollary differences in economic and social characteristics associated with homeownership. A major focus of social policy in this area should be on facilitating homeownership among young African Americans who may not have access to inherited family wealth which often provides the foothold needed to purchase one's first home. Significantly, this disadvantage affects African Americans at all educational and income levels. There are numerous social as well as economic benefits to homeownership, which should be afforded to African-American young adults at higher levels than is currently the case. Homeownership represents both an integral part of the American Dream, as well as a major component of wealth. As such, growing inequalities between blacks and white Generation X'ers with regards to homeownership should be a matter of pressing social concern.

References

Gans, Herbert J. 1988. *Middle American Individualism*. New York: The Free Press.

Farley, Reynolds. 2000. *The New American Reality: Who We Are, How We Got Here, Where Are We Going*. New York: Russell Sage Foundation.

Horton, Hayward D. 1992. "Race and Wealth: A Demographic Analysis of Black Homeownership." Sociological Inquiry 62:480-489.

Myers, Dowell and Julie Park. 1999. "The Role of Occupational Achievement in Homeownership Attainment by Immigrants and Native Born in Five Metropolitan Areas."

Myers, Dowell and Jennifer Wolch. 1995. "The Polarization of Housing Status" in State of the Union: America in the 1990's, vol. One: Economic Trends." Edited by Reynolds Farley. New York: Russell Sage.

Newman, Katherine. 1993. *Declining Fortunes: The Withering of the American Dream*. New York: Basic Books.

Oliver, Melvin L., and Thomas M. Shapiro. 1995. *Black Wealth/White Wealth: A New Perspective on Racial Inequality*. New York: Routledge.

Office of Policy Development and Research. 2000. "Homeownership: Progress and Work Remaining." U.S. Department of Housing and Urban Development.

U.S. Bureau of the Census. 1990. Statistical Abstracts of the United States. Washington D.C: U.S. Department of Commerce.

Wilson, William J. 1987. *The Truly Disadvantaged*. Chicago: The University of Chicago Press.

Table 2: Logistic Regression of Homeownership Attainment, 1980-2000

Variables	1980		1990		2000	
	Model 1	Model 2	Model 1	Model 2	Model 1	Model 2
Race	0.35	0.77	0.35	0.73	0.31	0.55
Age	-----	1.14	-----	1.20	-----	1.10
Marital status	-----	4.05	-----	2.40	-----	1.44
Education						
High school graduate	-----	1.38	-----	1.21	-----	0.81
Some college	-----	1.30	-----	1.05	-----	0.86
College graduate and beyond	-----	1.18	-----	0.93	-----	0.57
Region	-----	1.25	-----	1.24	-----	1.22
Income	-----	2.30	-----	2.47	-----	2.71
Race*marital status	-----	0.66	-----	0.69	-----	0.80
R-squared	0.02	0.18	0.03	0.17	0.03	0.14

Black Americans and the Internet: The Technological Imperative

BY JOEL DREYFUSS

The adoption of the Internet as a commercial medium probably came faster than any previous communications technology. While it took decades for the telephone or television to deeply penetrate the American home, the Internet—originally created for scientists to communicate in a national emergency—became a household word in less than five years. By mid-2000, according to a federal survey, more than half of all American homes had at least one computer and more than four in 10 homes had access to the Internet.

The Internet explosion was triggered by the creation of the Web "browser" in 1994, software that made it possible to easily view documents and images, hear audio and music and play video broadcasts over a personal computer. Thus, what had been an arcane technology used primarily for scholarly discussion and electronic correspondence was suddenly transformed into a form of mass media. And like all other new media that have emerged in the last few decades, the role of African Americans in this exciting new form of communications immediately came under scrutiny.

Early studies of U.S. participation in the Internet indicated that the initial users were overwhelmingly white and male. Just 11.8 percent of urban blacks had a computer in their homes, contrasted

131

with 30.3 percent of whites and 13.2 percent of Hispanics, said a 1999 report, "Falling Through the Net," by the National Telecommunications and Information Administration, a Commerce Department agency. "However," the report cautioned, "the rural poor are lowest in terms of *computer* penetration (4.5 percent) and—among those households with computers—*modem* (23.6 percent) penetration compared to central cities (7.6 percent and 43.9 percent) and urban areas (8.1 percent and 44.1 percent)." It may have been significant that the very first study suggested urban African Americans were not at the bottom of the heap in using this emerging technology. But the numbers alarmed some public advocates and leaders in the African-American community. With the Internet being touted as a treasure that would make vast amounts of information available even in the most remote villages and revolutionize industry, the opportunities seemed unlimited for those who were connected. Advocates of minorities and the poor began warning about the threat of a "digital divide," a nation divided among computer haves and computer have-nots and suggesting that another layer of inequality was being added to the already contentious ground between black and white, rich and poor, connected and unplugged.

It was a compelling story, even if there were already critics warning about the danger of seeing the glass half-empty instead of half-full. The response in the African-American community was in the style of previous social crises. Being defined by its pathologies has been the fate of African Americans for most of the twentieth century. In the traditional discovery and response form, sociological studies, criminal statistics, and commissions report shortcomings; civil rights institutions propose remedies. Public and private funding is applied to the problem. The debate about the "digital divide" took place on the watch of the Clinton Administration, much beloved by African Americans but, seemingly paradoxically, one of the most conservative Democratic governments in recent history. While the Administration expressed concern about the issue and proposed $2 billion in programs to help close the gap, even the Clintonites worried about federal interference in a new industry that was growing so quickly and becoming such a darling of the media.

There had been other visceral responses to media shortcomings. In the 1960s, the famed Kerner Commission Report pointed out the limited access of African Americans to the news media and, consequently, the distorted perceptions of blacks by most white Americans. This triggered a campaign to integrate the mass media, which opened the door for black journalists who had been largely excluded from major newspapers, magazines and networks. In the 1970s, an active communications lobby organized around access to the hot new field of cable television. The activists worried that inner-city neighborhoods would be bypassed by cable operators in pursuit of the most affluent audiences. In fact, many operators did—until they learned that dense inner-city neighborhoods were the most lucrative customers they could acquire.

In recent years, just how deep the digital divide is and how best to reduce it quickly became a subject of contention. Just months after the 1999 Commerce Department study reported the wide gap in Internet usage, private studies suggested the gap was not nearly as serious as believed—or that African Americans were closing the gap on their own. Forrester Research, a technology market research group, reported that African Americans were one of the fastest growing ethnic segments of Internet users—and that the gap would close by the year 2002. And setting the tone for the new Bush administration, Federal Communications Commission FCC Chair Michael Powell (son of Secretary of State Gen. Colin Powell) played down the digital divide by saying that while everyone may want a Mercedes-Benz, they couldn't necessarily have one.

While few will argue that owning a luxury car is a constitutional right, reasonable access to the Internet may well be a right of citizenship. No doubt, the Internet, like most earlier new media, was first propagated among the most affluent and those most closely allied with the mainstream of American power, knowledge and access, just as the telephone, radio and then television spread from the rich to the poor. Even well-off African Americans and Hispanics were using the Internet somewhat less than whites or Asians in its early days. But much of the gap, some studies suggested, could be attributed to less education and lower income. Also, the divide turned out to be an international issue: African and poor Asian nations were also missing out on the Internet. In some parts of Africa, there were as few as 6 personal computers per 100 people, compared to nearly 25 per 100 in the U.S.

The obsession with user penetration rates missed another aspect of black Internet use completely. It became a mantra that Asians ranked No.1 among Internet users, with whites second and blacks and Hispanics trailing. Yet, because of population differences, in absolute numbers there were more than three times as many African-American users of the Internet as Asians. The perception that African Americans were not on line in significant numbers was a useful lever for promoters of programs to narrow the Digital Divide. But it also had an impact in the early commercial exploitation of the Internet. Not surprisingly, the first wave of Internet sites and portals were aimed at the "mainstream" audience. If the site involved music, it tended to be white rock or California "new wave" mood music. Topics and categories rarely included topics that indicated a concern about a more diverse non-white audience. And investors often told entrepreneurs who wanted to set up sites for African Americans that "blacks are not on line." It set up a vicious cycle: there weren't many black-oriented sites and there wasn't much to draw African Americans to the Internet.

Commercial exploitation of the Internet would inflate the "technology bubble" of the late 1990s, creating great wealth, a plethora of new "Internet billionaires" and companies like Yahoo and Excite whose stock market values soared to unbelievable heights—only to crash virtually with the dawn of the new century. Few African Americans were involved in the new tech boom, not just as entrepreneurs but also as employees. Silicon Valley, in Northern California, was located in an area with a black population of just 5 percent. But Hispanics, a far greater presence, also landed few jobs in the industry. An investigation by the *San Francisco Chronicle* reported that just 4 percent of employees in Silicon Valley companies were African American and just 7 percent were Hispanic.

When news media—and subsequently, the Rev. Jesse Jackson—highlighted the racial disparities, it raised an uproar in Silicon Valley. The issue was a lack of technical education, not race, argued many of the Valley's defenders. No doubt, a technical education had been a requirement for admission in the early days of the tech boom. Not surprisingly, Asians and Asian Americans, highly represented in engineering and technical fields, were very visible in the new business. The same newspaper study reported that Asians and Asian Americans made up 31 percent of Silicon Valley employees. Several of the most visible early successes, including Yahoo and Hotmail, included Asian or Asian-American founders. Foreign funding was also a key; some startups found investors in Taiwan, Korea and India. India, with a large number of English-speaking technical graduates became a source of inexpensive programming talent for American industry. One result was that one in 4 Valley startups are run by Asians and Asian Americans.

However, a handful of black entrepreneurs and innovators have played significant roles in Silicon Valley from its earliest days. Roy Clay set up the first computer lab for Hewlett Packard and went on to build his own high-tech testing company, Rod-El. One of the founders of Silicon Graphics was Marc Hannah, who designed the graphics chip used in the powerful workstation.

Robert Knowling Jr. served as CEO of Covad, a provider of high-speed Internet service. John W. Thompson, a former IBM executive, is the chairman and CEO of Symantec, one of the largest U.S. software companies. African Americans have also held significant positions at Hewlett-Packard and Sun Microsystems. And there is a significant pool of minority talent, more than 100,000 blacks and 60,000 Hispanics hold degrees in engineering and science, according to Graland Thompson, editorial director at Career Communications, publisher of magazines for minority engineers. And another 7,000 graduate from universities each year.

Nonetheless, there's been little pressure for diversity in fiercely libertarian Silicon Valley. When the Rev. Jackson took up the issue in 1999, one of his most vocal critics was T.J. Rodgers, the president and CEO of Cypress Semiconductor, who warned against a lowering of standards. Rodgers cited his own diversified senior management staff. Unfortunately, his diversity was more the exception than the rule. A survey of 49 Silicon Valley companies showed just two blacks and one Hispanic among 364 board members in 1999.

One lesson in technology adoption is that old attitudes don't automatically disappear in new settings. In its early days, television was no more integrated than radio. When MTV was launched, the cable music network barred videos by black artists, initially explaining that they didn't meet MTV's "standards." In truth, MTV's founders probably wanted to recreate the segregated radio formats they knew from FM radio. That resistance quickly crumbled when black artists and labels objected loudly and drew attention to the policy. Today, black artists are a mainstay of MTV. Ironically, the man in charge at MTV during that controversy was Robert Pittman, now Co-Chief Operating Officer of AOL Time Warner.

In an eerie replay of older industries, the on-line delivery service, Kosmo.com, was accused in 2000 of red-lining when a newspaper story reported the company did not deliver in some affluent, but predominantly black, sections of Washington DC. The company argued that the delivery territory was determined by demographics—and crime rates—but much of their data turned out to be out-of-date. The dust-up soon became moot when Kozmo went out of business in early 2001.

For many African Americans, the Internet promised cost-free delivery of content. For a community traditionally underserved by news media, the Net offered a way to get targeted content to a selected audience without the associated costs of a traditional newspaper or magazine. The first major sites to be launched focused on news and information. NetNoir, in Northern California, and The Black World Today (www.tbwt.com) were among the first to appear. The Afro-American Newspapers chain, based in Baltimore, launched the first site by a traditionally black newspaper, initially focused on a series of dispatches and letters written by African-American reporters in World War II.

At first glance, the Internet would seem an appropriate vehicle for ethnic content. The Web has made it possible to put content on an individual's desktop without the waste of mass media delivery. You could reach a very selected audience and feed them advertising picked on the basis of their Internet browsing habits. Other ethnic groups explored the on-line options. Channel A was one of the first Asian-oriented sites, although it changed its goals several times during its existence. Several Hispanic-oriented sites emerged, in both Spanish and English, including El Puente and LatinFlava.ut the ad-based model, had unexpected limitations. Fledgling Web entrepreneurs found that while the delivery cost was close to zero, there were still substantial expenses for acquisition of content and the production and presentation of information. In short, writers, editors, photographers, designers and programmers all cost money. With advertisers slow to embrace the Web, African-American entrepreneurs found it difficult to raise money or to finance their efforts. Established black entrepreneurs stayed away from Internet investments in droves. The absence of capital limited the quality and breadth of many fledgling sites—and limited their ability to draw new audiences. And venture money was almost impossible to get. Bankers didn't know the African-American market and had little previous experience with black entrepreneurs.

The next wave of black-oriented Internet sites were financed largely through alliances with large corporations. NetNoir, which started as an incubation project at AOL, obtained additional financing to expand from just AOL to the Internet. Robert Johnson's BET launched a site in an agreement with Microsoft called MSBET; later, Johnson brought in additional backers and renamed the site BET.com. Rap entrepreneur Russell Simmons launched a Web site but soon sold it to BET. Harvard academic entrepreneur Henry Louis Gates launched Africana.com, but sold it to Time Warner. Barry Cooper's Black Voices was initially backed by the Tribune Company in Chicago.

Ironically, other than Bob Johnson's BET, the largest and best-financed black media companies have so far failed to make a mark in the Internet. While magazines like *Essence* and *Black Enteprise* posted rudimentary Web sites, they have up to now failed to be seen as major players in the new medium. Radio One, the largest black-owned radio network, was late to the Net. One exception was Granite Broadcasting, a network of nine TV stations led by founder and CEO Donald Cornwell. Cornwell jumped into the Net early, tying his stations together and providing additional content to support his TV news departments.

To get out of the "box" of ethnic media, minority-oriented companies have had to define themselves for a larger audience. One of the most successful is StarMedia, a site aimed not just at U.S. Hispanics, but at Spanish-speakers throughout Latin America. StarMedia was able to raise millions from venture funds and completed a successful IPO that created a company worth billions of dollars. Most of that value later vanished, but StarMedia set a standard of success for an ethnic media company.

Urban Box Office (UBO), where this author spent eight months as editor-in-chief, also tried to create a trans-racial business. While UBO's original content—text, video, animation and audio—was on the cutting edge of the urban sensibility and rooted in the black experience, the company touted its market as multi-racial. UBO customers were "first generation urban" and the company's ads showed young, black, white and Asians sharing common cultural experiences: a day at the beach, dancing, listening to music, doing each other's hair. UBO's model was the very successful *Vibe* magazine, which had black content, but was aimed at a multi-racial audience. Unfortunately, UBO never got to fully test its business model. When a fourth round of financing failed to materialize in the fall of 2000, the company, which had swelled to a staff of 300, shut its doors.

The prevailing view in the Internet business today is that so-called content sites are not financially viable. It is not just the minority sites that have failed; many of the largest mainstream sites have struggled to survive, from Pseudo.com to Inside.com to Salon.com. Some black-oriented Web sites suggest a different business model. Black Planet, a community site with an emphasis on chats, dating and free email, was successful in registering one million users in its first year. But despite a reasonable flow of readers, Black Planet has had difficulty attracting enough advertising revenue to guarantee its existence. Black Voices, which has gradually shifted to an emphasis on employment opportunities, suggests another model. However, Cooper and the Tribune Company have unsuccessfully sought additional investment for some time.

Furthermore, the stunning meltdown of technology stocks over the past year underscores the importance to African Americans of considering whether the Internet will support pure content sites that don't have the luxury of an affluent corporate backer. Some content sites continue to survive on a shoestring; but their content is limited because the editors can't afford to pay for quality content.

Indeed, even the viability of the Internet as a business has now come into question. The Net, some pundits say, may not be a business; it is just a vehicle for some businesses and it works best as a source of information. For African Americans who dreamed of the Web as a new Freedom's Journal, the results so far have been disappointing. So where is the so-called digital divide? As Adam Clayton Powell III, of the Freedom Forum, pointed out in *Reason* magazine in 2000, recent data from Forrester and Nielsen suggest that heavy government intervention may not be needed. According to Forrester, "Hispanic Americans were slightly ahead of white Americans in computer use earlier this year, and African Americans were closing the black-white gap at a rate that could lead to parity within the next 12 months. In terms of Internet use, the truly disadvantaged may well be Native Americans, who were not covered by the federal report."

It is important to note that the gap has been narrowed by the simple dynamics of our society. African Americans responded to the issue at both policy and personal levels. While the furor raged about the forms and limits of government intervention, black families responded to the debate as other groups had. They bought computers to assure their children would not be left behind, for their home businesses and for their own use. Also, the issue of the divide spurred private intervention. Many companies and organizations have invested in programs to close the gap. Organizations have wired poor urban schools for Internet access and provided equipment. Training programs have blossomed. While no one will argue that the gap is completely gone, the quick shift in numbers suggested that large segments of the minority community had not waited for government intervention or handouts; they had simply responded in their own self-interest.

The real digital divide may be among entrepreneurs. While many mainstream investors and entrepreneurs saw their paper billions disappear in the tech meltdown, few African Americans struck it rich to begin with. One of the few black-led firms to complete a public offering before the crash was DME Interactive Holdings, led by Darien Dash. In the early spring, when this article was written, the company's stock was selling for less than $1 a share.

What will become clear in the coming years is just what forms of Internet businesses make good businesses with a capacity to make a profit and grow. Those companies will have the best chances for long-term survival. African Americans and other ethnic groups must be prepared to take advantage of those opportunities as they emerge. The factors that will end the discussion of a Digital Divide are long-standing issues in the African-American community: better education, a promotion of entrepreneurial culture and access to capital.

Young African-American Men and Women: Separate Paths?

BY RUSSELL L. STOCKARD, JR.
AND M. BELINDA TUCKER

Increasingly, the paths of African-American men and women appear to be diverging. When examining social indicators for the race as a whole over the last thirty years, significant progress is evident in areas such as educational attainment, entry into high-status professions, middle-class status, and life expectancy. Yet, when viewed separately by sex, there are glaring differences between the apparent trajectory for males and females in a number of domains, including population size, schooling, income, occupation, marital behavior, living arrangements, criminal justice involvement and risk for HIV/AIDS. The differential experience of black women and men relative to some of these topics has received enormous attention in the media. Recall the oft-cited statistic that one of every three black men in his 20s is either incarcerated, on parole, or on probation (Mauer and Huling, 1995). A finding as dramatic as this one is highly suggestive of differences in other areas, including those that portend greater vulnerability to imprisonment (i.e., dropping out of high school) and those that result from being incarcerated, such as declines in future job prospects and health. Given the brevity of this report, we cannot report here on every area of interest, but we have selected those deemed critical by most observers. Also, this report focuses on young adults rather than the experience of children.

Although some results from the 2000 Census have been released, information broken down simultaneously by sex, race, and age is still largely unavailable. Therefore, the data presented and discussed in this chapter come largely from independent sources and the March 2000 Current Population Survey (CPS) which is an annual survey of a representative sample of the U.S. population conducted by the U.S. Census Bureau and the Bureau of Labor Statistics. The CPS is not as accurate as data from the 2000 Census (which attempts to assess the entire national population), but is generally viewed as a good estimate of the areas of interest.

Sex Ratio

According to the March 2000 CPS, there are just over 5 million black males ages 15 through 34 in the U.S. and nearly 5.7 million black females. The corresponding figures for the young adult population—ages 18 through 34—are 4 million and 4.8 million. The black sex ratio (i.e., the number of males for every 100 females) is therefore 89 for the age group 15-34 and 83 for those ages 18-34. This translates into a young adult population that is 46 percent male and 54 percent female. [It should be noted that these figures do overstate the disparity between the number of males and females, since young males are more likely to be missed in Census enumerations. Even with statistical "corrections" for the undercount, however, the overall black sex ratio has been low for the last fifty years. See Tucker and Mitchell-Kernan (1995) for a review.] Some social scientists have suggested that when the sex ratio for a group falls even slightly below 100, it can have dramatic social consequences, including a devaluing of marriage, more divorce and separation and more single-parent families (Guttentag and Secord, 1983). Though evidence that declining sex ratios have caused the changes in family patterns that are characteristic of African Americans today is equivocal, some studies do show the shortage of males to be linked to marriage and child-bearing behavior (Tucker and Mitchell-Kernan, 1995).

As important as the consequences of sex ratio imbalance is its cause. Differences in the total number of males compared to females are the result of higher male mortality across the entire life span (including the prenatal period) as well as an increasing invisibility of black men. Nationwide, Black men are making up an increasing proportion of the homeless population (as discussed below). These men are often missed in Census surveys. Finally, there are differences in the relative availability of men and women due to the differences in degrees of institutionalization (especially incarceration) of black men and women. As will be discussed later, the proportion of black males in prison is far greater than their overall representation in the general population.

This disparity in the numbers of young black men and women is a constant factor underlying many of the analyses presented throughout this chapter.

School Attendance and Educational Attainment

Scholars, politicians, and the public have long recognized the importance of education to the structure of opportunity, upward mobility, citizenship, and the mythologized American dream (Cohen and Nee, 2000). One area of significant change among African Americans over the last 40 years is the increase in educational attainment. African Americans are now far more likely to obtain both high school diplomas and college degrees than in previous decades. CPS estimates from March 2000 show that 85 percent of black men and 86 percent of black women age 20-35 graduated from high school (U.S. Bureau of the Census, 2000c). Among those ages 25-34, 18 percent of men and 20 percent of women earned bachelor's degrees from 4-year institutions. These figures demonstrate a fair degree of gender parity in high school and college completion. Black women, however, are nearly twice as likely as men to hold master's degrees (2.4 percent vs. 1.5 percent). The survey sample figures at higher educational levels are not as reliable (since they are based on relatively small numbers), but they suggest that while black women and men are equally likely to hold doctorates, more women now hold professional degrees.

Despite these figures, others have cited evidence among African Americans of "an increasing degree conference on females in the midst of declining, stagnating, and, at best, minimal increases in the educational achievements of their male counterparts" (Cohen and Nee, 2000). The current state of relative gender equality, then, also reflects a decrease in the representation of black men in college. It should be noted that some writers cite gender disparities in the proportion of degrees awarded to blacks (with greater proportions going to women) without accounting for the fact that there are significantly fewer men available to achieve these awards (referring back to the sex ratio imbalance).

The fact that women are more likely to hold Master's and professional degrees raises questions about what is happening with the men who are not pursuing such goals nor other advanced college degrees. These men may be choosing to enter the military rather than college programs (at least not directly), although women's representation has increased in that institution as well. In addition, the previously mentioned negative involvement of increasing numbers of black men in particular into the criminal justice system also plays a role.

Another possible explanation for the apparent sex differential among black degree holders is the attractiveness of "proprietary" schools to black men seeking promising careers. These schools include various kinds of career training programs, such as computer technologies, information sciences, law-related careers, and medical technologies. Some estimates suggest that more than 70 percent of new jobs in the new millennium will not require a college degree, making such proprietary schools an important component of the overall career preparation process for blacks. An analysis by the journal *Black Issues in Higher Education* (July 9, 2000) found that the top producer of baccalaureates for minorities in engineering-related technologies was a California campus of the ITT Technical Institute of California. The number two and three institutions conferring degrees in computer and information science on African Americans were also private career colleges—Strayer College and DeVry Institute of Technology.

Community college systems and proprietary schools are more accessible to those with limited funds, those who can only attend part time (due both to the need to work and family obligations), those who did not have the grades or standardized test scores required for 4-year institutions, and those who have not completed high school in traditional ways. Despite these attractions, the *Black Issues in Higher Education* analysis points out the drawbacks of obtaining such a specific rather than general education. That is, a more general education provides the flexibility to adapt to the rapid and often unforeseen changes occurring in today's job market.

Occupations

While much emphasis has been placed on women moving into formerly male occupational preserves, recent data reveal new developments for black men and women in the 18-34 year age span. First of all, the March 2000 CPS data demonstrates that there are more total women than men in both the 18 to 24 and the 24 to 34 age occupational categories (i.e., persons holding jobs) (U.S. Bureau of the Census, 2000d). We can surmise that the younger category encompasses those persons who have not yet received or will not receive post-secondary education or training, while the older category should be comprised mainly by those who have. In the younger category, there are 908,000 black men and 1,089,000 black women. In the second category, black women outnumber men by 2,074,000 to 1,734,000. Recall, though, that there are fewer men in this age category.

An inspection of the occupational subcategories discloses a larger number of black women in almost every case—often far in excess of their numerical advantage. In the 18 to 24 year age range, the exceptions are the somewhat less prestigious and, in some cases, also lower paying occupational categories, including: private household service; other service; precision, crafts, and repair; machine operators, assembly, and inspectors; transport and material moving; handlers and laborers; and farmers, forestry, and fishing. This pattern repeats itself in the 25 to 34 year age range. For example, there were 169,000 black men age 25-34 in the transport and material moving category, compared to 41,000 black women. A number of these categories do pay quite a bit more than the sales, administrative, and technical support jobs dominated by women.

In the younger age range, African-American women are more numerous than men in the executive, administrative, and managerial occupations, 41,000 to 31,000; in the professional occupations 80,000 to 50,000; and in the technical areas, 40,000 to 16,000. In the older age range, the pattern of black female numerical advantage continues in the managerial occupations 230,000 to 174,000; in the professional occupations 292,000 to 173,000; and in the technical area 73,000 to 36,000.

In a service and knowledge-based economy, the representation of younger black women bodes well for them as they stand to share in the growth of services sector and in professions requiring knowledge to advance. At the same time, the pattern of black female numerical advantage in contrast to black men carries a number of implications for the African-American community. Among these are suggestions that mate selection and marriage may be affected, that the management and the professions may come to be seen as "women's work," and that African-American men may not choose to enter these occupational categories. The root cause of these discrepancies is a more complex issue, given that educational attainment of young black adult men and women is not nearly as distinct (though black women are more likely to obtain master's level degrees that may facilitate entry into the higher administrative ranks). It may also be the case that African-American women are not seen as direct competitors by white males, who still largely control the corporate structure, and can more easily than black men move into these more prestigious positions.

Income

Despite the apparent occupational advantages of young black women over black men in many areas, income statistics reveal a different picture. In March 2000 the median income for non-Hispanic black men age 25-34 was $27,748 compared to $24,166 for non-Hispanic black women. This may be explained in part by certain of the observations made above in the occupational section. That is, men are more likely to hold certain skilled occupations that, though often viewed as less prestigious, may pay more than the administrative support and sales jobs that are held by so many black women.

Table 1 displays median income for young adults by education levels. (The sample sizes for Master's degrees and above are too small for presentation.) The gender differential varies quite substantially depending on years of schooling, and is most striking for persons who have high school diplomas but no additional education as well as for those with at least a bachelor's degree. It appears that a terminal degree has less value for young black women.

Poverty indicators demonstrate a similar pattern. Data from 1999 show that in the age group 18-24, 21.5 percent of black men

Table 1. Median Income in 1999 by Educational Attainment: Black Non-Hispanic Men and Women Age 25-34: March 2000

	Total	Not High School Graduate	High School Graduate or GED	Some College, No Degree	Associate Degree	Bachelor's Degree or More
Men	$27,748	$17,058	26,781	$26,165	$26,577	$37,968
Women	$24,166	$16,860	$18,660	$24,463	$25,774	$31,871

Source: U.S. Bureau of the Census (2000), Table 8.

compared to 31.6 percent of black women had incomes below the poverty level (Bureau of Labor Statistics and U.S. Bureau of the Census, 2000). In the later years of young adulthood, more people held jobs since most have completed their educational pursuits. Yet, even at ages 25-34, 8.9 percent of black men were living below the poverty level, but nearly a quarter of black women (24 percent) were impoverished. In addition to the fact that U.S. women overall still earn less than men, the greater poverty among black women may also reflect their increased responsibility for the rearing of children as single parents. That is, the women are more likely to be in households with multiple persons dependent on a single, limited income.

Marital Status and Living Arrangements

One possible factor in what appears to be a growing separateness of the experiences of African-American women and men is the decline in marriage evident over the past several decades (Tucker and Mitchell-Kernan, 1995). Table 2 displays marital status for African-American men and women ages 18-24 and ages 25-34. Although for African Americans as a whole, men are more likely to be married than women—36.2 percent versus 28.9 percent (U.S. Bureau of the Census, 1999), among younger blacks, marital patterns of men and women are now quite similar in most respects. These trends reflect increasing tendencies for African Americans to delay marriage, to divorce, and to remain single (Tucker, 2000). Note that 9 percent of men and over 13 percent of women in the 25-34-age bracket are divorced or separated. These are fairly substantial figures, given that most persons in that age group have never married.

Though these figures are indicative of a decline in legal marriage, they do not mean that young men and women are living completely separate lives. Surveys of African Americans do indicate that most young men and women are romantically involved.

However, one area of clear difference between the sexes that has remained is the greater tendency of African-American men to date and marry persons of other races (Taylor, Tucker and Mitchell-Kernan, under review). Recent newspaper accounts of independently analyzed March 2000 CPS data show that black men are still about 3 times more likely to marry someone of another race than are black women.

In terms of living arrangements, one area of stark contrast between men and women is the extent to which they are homeless.

Table 2. Marital Status for Young Non-Hispanic Black Men and Women (Percents): March 1999

	Married, Spouse Present	Married, Spouse Absent	Widowed	Divorced	Separated	Never Married
Men 18-24	5.6	.4	-	.7	1.7	91.6
Women 18-24	6.8	.3	-	.9	2.6	89.3
Men 25-34	34.0	2.1	-	6.0	3.3	54.7
Women 25-34	31.6	1.9	.9	6.1	7.2	52.3

Source: U.S. Bureau of the Census (2000c)

Though complete and accurate data are hard to come by, given the nature of the population, an annual report on hunger and homelessness conducted by the U.S. Conference of Mayors is an important and rare source of information. The 2000 survey of 25 cities showed that African Americans constitute between 80-89 percent of the homeless in Chicago, Detroit, Norfolk, Philadelphia, St. Louis, and Trenton, NJ (The United States Conference of Mayors, 2000). There is no age breakdown in the data reports, but the 1998 Mayors survey found that most of the homeless in that sample of 30 cities were between 30 and 50 years old. And though the number of families among the homeless is increasing, the proportion of men is substantially greater than that of women in all cities. Overall, single men make up 44 percent of the homeless population. Since the report attributes much of the blame for the increase in homelessness to the lack of affordable housing, the population of young African-American adults is at risk for such a plight, especially as the economy weakens.

Criminal Justice Involvement

There has been an explosive increase in the rate of incarceration in this country. Between 1990 and 1999, the number of persons over-all in U.S. prisons and jails increased by 712,000, which represents an annual increase of 5.8 percent (Beck, 2000). At the beginning of the decade, 1 in every 218 U.S. residents was in jail or prison. By 1999, that ratio had become 1 of every 147. This unprecedented growth is large-ly the result of the far more punitive laws and sentencing require-ments adopted at both state and federal levels, as well as the contro-versial "War on Drugs" (Mauer, 1990; Hawkins and Herring, 2000).

Unfortunately, young African-American men are bearing the brunt of this new offensive (see Table 3, on page 156). Hawkins and Herring (2000), among others, have cited the "racialization" of drug statutes and arrests, perhaps most visibly symbolized by the disparity between sentences required for crack cocaine and powder cocaine (with use and sales of the former being more prevalent in black communities). (See also Russell, 1998.) The Bureau of Justice national report on inmates at midyear 1999 reveals that fully 11 percent of black non-Hispanic males in their twenties and early thirties were incarcerated in 1999 (Beck, 2000). Among black males age 25 to 29, 12.3 percent of the total population was in prison or jail; compared to 4.2 percent of Hispanic/Latino men and only 1.5 percent of white men.

Black women are far less likely to be incarcerated than black men. Those in jail or prison represent less than 1 percent of the black female young adult population. Overall, the number of incarcerated young black men is 11 times the number of young women. Yet, the same ethnic pattern can be observed. That is, in 1999 black women were 2.5 times more likely than Hispanic women and 7 times more likely than white women to be incarcerated (Beck, 2000). As shown in Table 4 (on page, 157) although the peak age among black men for incarceration is the 25-29 age group, for all groups of women the incarceration rate peaks in the early 30s.

With more states passing three strikes laws and other statutes that assure longer terms of incarceration as well as the increasingly conservative orientation of the judiciary, these trends show no signs of abatement.

HIV/AIDS

Perhaps the most devastating health crisis faced this century by the African-American population is Acquired Immune Deficiency Syndrome (AIDS). A disparity between men and women has been apparent from the earliest days of the epidemic, but the gender gap is being narrowed by rapidly increasing infection rates among women. As of June 2000, 78,479 cases of AIDS had been diagnosed in black males under the age of 35 compared to 34,791 women of the same age (Center for Disease Control and Prevention, 2000b, Table 7). Deaths from AIDS reported through the same date included 33,233 black males and 11,659 black females under the age of 35 (CDC, 2000b, Table 19). Although the 14,103 black males of all ages who were diagnosed with AIDS in 1999 were most likely to have been exposed to HIV through sex with other men (42 percent), another third were infected through drug use (CDC, 2000b, Table 20). This contrasts sharply with white male infection routes, which have tended to be overwhelmingly from sex with other men (71 percent).

A recent CDC report (CDC, 2000a) suggests that black and Hispanic men who have sex with men (MSM) differ from white MSMs in some important ways that have implications for the discussion at hand. First, data from 1989-1998 show that among men who have sex with men and were diagnosed with HIV or AIDS, the proportion who are young (age 13-24) is higher among minorities than among whites. Second, a CDC study of 8,780 MSMs with HIV infection or AIDS determined that black men who have sex with men were more likely than others to identify themselves as heterosexual: 24 percent of blacks compared to 15 percent of Hispanics, 11 percent of Asian/Pacific Islander Americans and 6 percent of non-Hispanic whites.

These statistics have grave implications for African-American women's risk of HIV infection, since they indicate that black women have a greater chance than other women of encountering a male partner who is infected with HIV. This fear is borne out by the data. African-American women now have a higher incidence of AIDS than any other group of women in the U.S., accounting for 63 percent of the total number of women diagnosed with AIDS in 1999. Moreover, young adulthood appears to be the period at greatest risk of contracting AIDS for black women—42 percent of all diagnoses occurred from ages 20-34. Of the 6,539 black women who were diagnosed with AIDS in 1999, 64 percent were infected through heterosexual intercourse and one-third were exposed through injecting drug use (CDC, 2000b, Table 21).

Summary and Policy Implications

These data show some significant disparities in the situation and well-being of young adult African-American women and men. Within these groups, black women currently outnumber black men. Although they graduate from high school and college and hold doctorates in virtually equal proportions, women are more likely to hold master's and professional degrees. Young black women hold more professional, administrative, and clerical jobs, while black men hold more skilled trades and heavy machinery related positions. Young black women with terminal degrees make less money than similarly qualified young black men. Black men are greatly over-represented in prisons and jails and the number of black women with HIV/AIDS has increased quite dramatically.

What we make of these differences depends largely on the particular nature of each. This kind of in-depth analysis (including trends over time, direction of change, contextual factors, etc.) is beyond the scope of this brief report, though some problems are self-evident. Improvement in health practices, particularly prevention programs, are needed to address both the high mortality of African-American men generally and the incredibly high HIV/AIDS risk for both men and women. This will require involvement by every major sector of African-American communities, including schools, churches, community groups, etc. The unacceptably high incarceration rate of young African Americans, especially men, must be addressed through new prevention programs as well as directed attacks on the regressive legislation that unnecessarily criminalizes huge segments of the black population. Though this report has not examined the overall economic climate for young African Americans, the gender-based income differences and the enduring high levels of impoverishment among women in particular suggest the need for new economic development strategies. That is, major sections of the African-American population have not benefited from the economic growth of the last few years. Given the severe changes in welfare law, the recent economic downturn may spell disaster for many of these people. New affordable housing developments are crucial for addressing both the needs of impoverished more generally and many homeless persons (though improved mental health care is also needed for some). Finally, as we begin this new century, support for families is a more critical need than ever, given the array of risks faced. In other writings we have addressed this need more fully (see Tucker, 2000). Suffice it to state here that a greater investment in the welfare of African-American families (including child-care, educational needs, health needs, etc.) will have enormous payoffs for this society in general.

Table 3. Number of Young Adult Inmates in State or Federal Prisons Local Jails by Age, Race and Gender: June 30, 1999

Age	Male				Female			
	Total	Black	Latino	White	Total	Black	Latino	White
18–19	78,600	35,300	16,000	24,400	3,700	1,400	500	1,700
20–24	298,600	136,200	62,000	91,400	18,800	7,200	3,900	7,200
25–29	316,800	152,200	59,600	96,000	28,700	13,200	4,700	9,600
30–34	320,700	142,300	55,700	114,400	37,300	18,900	4,900	12,600

Source: Beck (2000), Table 12 (p. 10).

Table 4. Number of Young Adult Inmates in State or Federal Prisons Local Jails per 100,000 Residents by Age, Race and Gender: June 30, 1999

Age	Male				Female			
	Total	Black	Latino	White	Total	Black	Latino	White
18–19	1,868	5,787	2,524	885	92	224	94	63
20–24	3,130	10,407	4,141	1,462	205	524	284	121
25–29	3,363	12,334	4,220	1,535	303	956	357	154
30–34	3,193	11,225	3,844	1,674	370	1,362	372	185

Source: Beck (2000), Table 13 (p. 10).

References

Beck, Allen J. 2000. *Prison and Jail Inmates at Midyear 1999.* Bureau of Justice Statistics Bulletin. Washington, DC: U.S. Department of Justice, Office of Justice Programs.

Black Issues in Higher Education. July 9, 2000. Proprietary Preference For-profit colleges gain momentum in producing graduates of color. Reprinted at <http://www.phdproject.org/phd13.html>

Bureau of Labor Statistics and U.S. Bureau of the Census. 2000. Current Population Survey, Annual Demographic Survey, March Supplement. Table 1: Age, Sex, Household Relationship, Race and Hispanic Origin—Poverty Status of People with Selected Characteristics in 1999. <http://ferret.bls.census.gov/macro/032000/pov/new01_001.htm>

Center for Disease Control and Prevention (January 14, 2000a). HIV/AIDS Among Racial/Ethnic Minority Men Who Have Sex with Men—United States, 1989-1998. *Morbidity and Mortality Weekly Report,* 49(1), 4-11.

Center for Disease Control and Prevention (December, 2000b). *HIV/AIDS Surveillance Report,* Vol. 12 (1).

Cohen, Cathy J., and Claire E. Nee. 2000. Educational attainment and sex differentials in African American communities. *The American Behavioral Scientist.* 43, 1159-1206.

Guttentag, Marcia, Paul M. Secord. 1983. *Too Many Women: The Sex Ratio Question.* Beverly Hills: Sage Publications.

Hawkins, Darnell F., and Cedric Herring. 2000. Race, Crime, and Punishment: Old Controversies and New Challenges. In James S. Jackson (Ed.). *New Directions: African Americans in a Diversifying Nation.* Washington, DC: National Policy Association & University of Michigan Program for Research on Black Americans.

Mauer, Marc. 1990. Young Black Men and the Criminal Justice System: A Growing National Problem. Washington, DC: The Sentencing Project.

Mauer, Marc Tracy Huling. 1995. Young Black Men and the Criminal Justice System: Five Years Later. Washington, DC: The Sentencing Project.

Russell, Katheryn K. 1998. *The Color of Crime: Racial Hoaxes, White Fear, Black Protectionism, Police Harassment, and Other Macroaggressions.* New York: New York University Press.

The United States Conference of Mayors. 2000. Status Report on Hunger and Homelessness in America's Cities. <http://www,usmayors.org>

Taylor, Pamela, M. Belinda Tucker and Claudia Mitchell-Kernan (under review). Taylor, P. L., Tucker, M. B., & Mitchell-Kernan, C. Interethnic Dating and Marriage in 21 U.S. Cities.

Tucker, M. Belinda. 2000. Considerations in the Development of Family Policy for African Americans. In James S. Jackson (Ed.). *New Directions: African Americans in a Diversifying Nation.* Washington, DC: National Policy Association & University of Michigan Program for Research on Black Americans.

Tucker, M. Belinda and Claudia Mitchell-Kernan. 1995. *The Decline in Marriage Among African Americans: Causes, Consequences, and Policy Implications.* Newbury Park, CA: Russell Sage Foundation.

U.S. Bureau of the Census (2000a). Table 1. Age, Sex, Household Relationship, Race and Hispanic Origin—Poverty Status of People by Selected Characteristics in 1999. <http://ferret.bls.census.gov/macro/032000/pov/new01_001.htm>

U.S. Bureau of the Census (2000b). Educational Attainment in the United States: March 2000, Detailed Tables. Table 8: Income in 1999 by Educational Attainment for People 18 years Old and Over, by Age, Sex, Race and Hispanic Origin: March 2000. <http://www.census.gov/population/www/socdemo/education/p20-536.html>

U.S. Bureau of the Census (2000b). Educational Attainment in the United States: March 2000, Detailed Tables. Table 1a. Percent of High School and College Graduates of the Population 15 Years and over, by Age, Sex, Race and Hispanic Origin: March 2000. <http://www.census.gov/population/www/socdemo/education/p20-536.html>

U.S. Bureau of the Census (2000d). Educational Attainment in the United States: March 2000, Detailed Tables. Table 6. Educational Attainment of Employed Civilians 18-64 Years, by Occupation, Age, Sex, Race, and Hispanic Origin: March 2000. <http://www.census.gov/population/www/socdemo/education/p20-536.html>

U.S. Bureau of the Census (1999). Table 1. Selected Social Characteristics of the Population, by Sex, Region, and Race: March 1998. <http://www.census.gov/population/socdem/race/Black/tabs98/tab01.txt>

Young Adults and the Appearance of Religion

REVEREND MARK V.C. TAYLOR

Religion is alive and well in the homes, worship houses and hearts of many African-American young adults. As a working definition, I take religion to mean: a system of belief in, and worship of, a Supreme Being (or Beings). This system produces communities, institutions, and organizations that seek to shape the life of the individuals and groups within it.

The title of this article is metaphorical. "Appearance" alludes to Ralph Ellison's metaphor of the invisibility of black people in this society. *Religion, as a mode of acquiring personal and collective power, has the ability to make its adherents "appear," i.e. be seen or even become more real, to themselves, and to those who would make them invisible.* The metaphor of "appearance" also means that this attempt to give both an overview without claiming to be definitive or exhaustive. Other interpretations are possible. I do hope however, to facilitate an understanding of religion as it attracts young black adults, ages 25-35.

The Dominant Expressions: Christianity

Currently, the dominant religion in the African-American community is Christianity; taken together, its seven major black denominations—the African Methodist Episcopal, the African Methodist Episcopal Zion, the Christian Methodist Episcopal, the

Church of God in Christ, the National Baptist Convention, USA, the National Baptist Convention, Inc., and the Progressive National Baptist Convention—claim a membership of more than 25 million members. To these, one could also add several other smaller denominations, as well as black constituencies in white denominations; and, at the cutting edge of the black Church movement," the mega ministries movement.

Mega ministries are rooted in megachurches, the large congregations of three thousand and more members which have developed since the 1970s. One point of difference between these new megachurches and older megachurches is that much of the latter's membership comes from the new African-American middle class which rushed through the new doors of opportunity opened by the Civil Rights and Black Power struggles of the 1960s.

Another is these newer megachurches' focus on the concept of "ministry."

Although I can't pinpoint the emergence of this term, I personally associate it with the rise of the ministry of Reverend Fred Price, pastor of the Crenshaw Christian Center, in Los Angeles In the 1980s. Rev. Price spurred a revolution in African-American Christianity with his emphasis on the "Word," (i.e., the Bible) in his own "word ministry"—which included a popular TV show, evangelistic tours, and national conferences. Although ministries emphasizing spiritual and material prosperity were not new, the demographic character of the majority of Price's congregants was a new element: They were a new black middle class seeking religious understandings and undergirdings of the prosperity which stemmed from their inclusion in the mainstream corporate and government worlds. Many of those deeply influenced by Price's "Word" revolution were black adults, ages 25-35.

This concept of ministry was part of a doctrine of truth grounded in Protestant evangelical Christianity, which holds the *Bible* as the ultimate authority for both group and individual life. This concept of ministry said that for every human need there is a foundation of effective, applicable truth in the *Bible*. Out of this doctrine, "singles," "couples," "men's," and "women's," ministries began to emerge. The combination of new doctrinal interpretations and emphases, national media and effective examples that converged in ministries like Rev. Price's have had a powerful appeal to young adults grappling with the stresses of life in the post-technological era. Many, if not most of these newer mega churches are Pentecostal or neo-Pentecostal. This is an important feature because Pentecostalism promotes a relationship with God and an expression of one's religious fervor that is both intensely individualistic and simultaneously communal. That is, Pentecostalism insists on the necessity of the individual being filled with the Holy Spirit—and producing evidence of that filling, usually by speaking in an unknown tongue. Thus, the size of the megachurches, which brings together thousands and thousands of individuals who believe in *expressing their religious fervor in public ways*, gives them the potential to significantly affect the economic, political and social tone of their communities by shaping religious expression across geographical, gender, class and sometimes even racial, lines. That is an immense potential, as one can see from considering the current major figure in the mega-ministry movement: Bishop T.D. Jakes. Much has been written about him. Most important for this discussion, however, is the fact that his $20 million ministry, his 26,000 member church, with its sanctuary which holds 8,000 worshippers, his $135 million housing development financed by his church—are all ministries based on need.

Bishop Jakes came to national prominence and ecclesiastical power, as the teacher and preacher of the "Woman Thou Art Loosed" series. This was first a sermon, next a Sunday school class, followed by a set of conferences and tapes, then a musical CD and culminating with a theatrical drama. The genius of this effort is that it creatively addressed an under-investigated problem in the

African-American community—the emotional pain of black women besieged by the problems of life in the decades after the great civil rights victories. Whether it was the pain of poor working or unemployed women stemming from low wages or no wages, or the pain of upper- and middle-class women originating from their sojourn through institutions and corporations tainted by white-supremacist thought and practice, this pain has been intensely felt, but not often specifically addressed in many black churches. Black women ages 25-35, like all black women and girls, are plagued by the worst features of African-American life: teen age pregnancy and its subsequent poverty; the absence of black "marriageable" men; domestic violence and rape; the re-emergence and growth of a street value system that demeans, denigrates and destroys woman-hood, and the "anti-sisterhood" friction caused by the suppression of notions of African female beauty.

Focusing on such specific needs has also led mega-ministries to address the absence of young black males from Christian church-es. Here, too, Bishop Jakes has taken the lead in establishing men's seminars, books and conferences. Other Christian leaders such as Bishop Eddie Long in Atlanta, whose church is 43-percent male, have been successful in turning religious words, rites and relation-ships into elements that draw black males. At a time where homi-cide is the number one killer of black males between 15 and 34, and suicide is the second biggest killer, the value of such male-based ministries cannot be overstated.

Such other megachurches as the Salem Baptist Church of Chicago, pastored by Rev. James T. Meeks, meet other needs of young adults, ages 25-35. A church member said that during a wor-ship service a person informed Reverend Meeks that a shooting was taking place outside the church. When the suggestion was made that the minister call for police involvement, he commanded that all the men in the 3,000-seat sanctuary follow him outside and stop the shooting themselves, with the explanation that male church members could solve such community problems on their own.

Such events in Salem are no fluke. The 17,000-member church successfully spearheaded the effort to vote the community "dry in" an anti-liquor referendum. Members walk the streets at night, in organized campaigns to "witness" to prostitutes, pimps and drug dealers. Meeks, the vice president of People United to save Humanity (PUSH), was present when Jesse Jackson arranged the release of three prisoners captured in Macedonia, in 1999.

Salem Church has a radio and television ministry, a bookstore and holds casual dress, up-tempo worship services. In the context of the church's religious activism, all these elements satisfy the need for people to have a model of valiant struggle against over-whelming odds.

This need for African-American heroism, is repressed by the stereotypical demonization of blacks in larger society, therefore its satisfaction in a mega church is all the more important.

In their seminal work, *The Church in the Black Experience*, C. Eric Lincoln and Lawrence Mayima show that one of the challenges that black churches face is to overcome the negative self-identifi-cation and racial ambivalence that still exists in the black commu-nity. Megaministries in the Christian community have dealt with this need also. One of the best examples of this is the West Angeles Church of God In Christ, under the leadership of Bishop Charles Blake, a faith community which represents the intersection of evangelical Pentecostalism, African-American culture and American society.

Bishop Blake's message emphasizes faith in the power of God to bring triumph and transcendence in this life and the next. Earlier this year, he led his 20,000-member congregation into its new $65 million structure. In a neighborhood where the church has been the backbone of $100 million worth of area redevelopment, it will be a demonstration of the truth of this message. West Angeles has over 80 ministries designed to meet a broad array of human needs, from singles ministries to ministries designed to help entrepreneurs start their own businesses.

Bishop Blake is on the Governing Board of the Church of God In Christ, (COGIC), whose membership of 5,500,000 members and growth rate of 836 percent during the last ten years make it the fastest growing of all the major black denominations. As the bishop of a jurisdiction in southern California, he oversees 250 churches in southern California.

West Angeles has become no less Pentecostal, while attracting a diverse congregation which includes celebrities such as Denzel Washington, Stevie Wonder, and Earvin "Magic" Johnson, Angela Basset, Courtney B. Vance and Lynn Whitfield. In West Angeles, black Hollywood, black rhythm and blues, and black basketball, three dominant streams of black culture, stir in the bosom of the leading church in black holiness-Pentecostal tradition.

In short, Bishop Blake and West Angeles, address the need to overcome negative racial self identification, by showing that one can be a black, Holy Ghost filled, successful Christian, making the most of one's own dream, while not forgetting the nightmares of the least of these (i.e., the most needy people). For many young adults ages 25-35, who are trying to overcome individual isolation, and embrace personal and group intimacy, or find a career and begin to chart their future, megaministries like West Angeles provide a comfortable home.

Critics of the mega ministries movement argue that doctrinal errors, gross materialism and ineffective social strategies, mar its effectiveness. These critiques must be weighed on their own merits. It does seem clear, however, that many young adults gravitate to these churches and ministries to help fill their physical, spiritual and social needs.

In addition to the emergence and growth of the mega ministries, another cutting-edge development within Christianity is the blossoming of hip hop gospel, of which the central figure is Kirk Franklin. In the way that Thomas Dorsey mixed spiritual music with the blues to create gospel music and as James Cleveland mixed gospel music with rhythm and blues (R&B) to shape contemporary gospel, so Franklin has been at the forefront of the merger of gospel with hip-hop music.

The difference is that hip hop is a much stranger partner to black Christian music than rhythm and blues, or even classic blues. Hip-hop's "gangsta" rap glamorizes, extols and encourages murder and violence. Its themes insult women and celebrate substance abuse.

Franklin avoids the worst characteristics of hip hop. His lyrics come out of evangelical Christian beliefs that endorse miracles, the reality of the devil, the need for salvation from Jesus Christ and the power of praise. The music is characterized by thudding, earthy, almost hypnotic rhythms. Franklin and his accompanying choirs dance to rhythms closer to party and club life than to the typical "holy dancing" of the church. If older adults listen closely, they will hear strains from Parliament Funkadelic's *One Nation Under A Groove* in Franklin's 1997 hit, *Stomp*. Indeed, he has been heavily criticized for ransacking secular music in this fashion and for making records with known hip-hop artists like R. Kelly. However, critics often overstate their case. Most of Franklin's music since 1993 has been closer to the dominant forms of black contemporary gospel, than to R&B or hip hop.

Not since M.C. Hammer's, neo-Christian, anti-drug album of 1990, *Too Legit To Quit*, has Christian music received such a reception from the non-Christian music world. Franklin has appeared on MTV, on Showtime at the Apollo and in television commercials. Franklin's success helped pave the way for other gospel artists, Fred Hammond and Yolanda Adams, who toured with him nationally. Hammond was the first gospel artist to record a double CD in 1998, taking praise and devotional gospel hip hop to new heights.

167

Yolanda Adams created a stir in mass black culture circles in 1999, with her rendition of *I Open Up My Heart* and several other popular recordings. Franklin and Adams in particular have been played on R&B and even hip-hop stations. Hammond went on to produce, direct and star in gospel plays.

Along with hip-hop gospel, there has been a proliferation of gospel rap, gospel dance, gospel drama, gospel jazz, gospel supper and comedy clubs and even gospel house music. This amounts to the creation of an alternative black Christian entertainment culture. This alternative black Christian entertainment culture is both linked to, and separate from, the dominant popular culture. It is by and for young adults, (Franklin himself is 31,) and it meets the recreational and cultural needs of those Christian young adults, who feel popular black secular culture, especially music, movies and comedy, is too often immoral and irrelevant.

Before moving away from Christianity we must mention those black Christian churches outside of the recent megachurch movement. These churches have many forms. They include the old-line giants, like Bethel AME Church in Philadelphia, and Mother AME Zion Church, Abyssinian Baptist Church and Concord Baptist Church, all in New York. In this group are the large churches and the storefront churches, born in the Great Migration northward, after World War II. Under current circumstances, the average black church has approximately 200 members, is congregational in polity and evangelical in practice. This group includes some neighborhood-based churches and others that are family-based, and even others steeped primarily in music ministry.

Two qualified generalizations may be applied to all of these churches. Of the churches that might be called traditionalist, custom is a salient feature and its leaders are not quick to modify long-held practices to accommodate young adults. Other churches might be called transformists. They recognize the need to change to keep or attract young adults. Noting the absence of adults ages 25-35, transformist leaders reexamine their doctrine and practice. They study what is working in other places and try to make changes in their congregations. Traditionalists and transformists are terms that apply not only to churches, but also apply to individuals.

The national picture is made more complex because some transformist individuals are in traditionalist churches and some traditionalist individuals are in transformist churches. Where traditionalists are in power, young adults often leave churches or religions rather than stay and contest prohibitions against praise dancers, praise and worship songs, drums and gospel rap, gospel skating, seminars on sex and relationships, and singles ministries. Where transformists are in power, and help move a church toward the recognition for change in order to, it attracts young adults.

The Dominant Expressions: Islam

The Nation of Islam (NOI) continues to be a potent force beyond its numerical strength, especially on the symbolic and political levels. It's Million Man March of 1995 has mushroomed into the Million March Movement, featuring the Million Woman March, the Million Youth March, the Million Youth Movement, and the Million Family March. Although debates abound as to the specific number in each of these marches, taken together, they have certainly enlisted over one million people and have received the support of many more. The Nation of Islam was financially rebuilt between the 1970s and 1990s largely by Minister Louis Farrakhan's speeches on college campuses, exposing a new religious militancy to many young adults.

The political significance of Minister Farrakhan and The Nation of Islam stems from the activity of its members in Black communities and its prominence in the national media. The Nation's members have been at the forefront of the fight against the drug trade in black communities, and their prison ministries security forces are well known. Although the entrepreneurial

169

empire of the Honorable Elijah Muhammad (including grocery and clothing stores, farms, and restaurants) has largely disappeared, Muslim men still sell newspapers and bean pies throughout many black communities. For many young adults who were too young to witness the courage and daring of Christians in the Civil Rights Movement, the perceived pacifism and lassitude of many Christian church members seems vastly inferior to these activist Muslim activities.

The mainstream media heightens the symbolic importance of The Nation because of its obsession with Minister Farrakhan's critique of Jewish power in the United States and the latent fear in the collective unconsciousness of many whites of a vengeful black horde seeking reprisals for the evils of slavery, segregation and social oppression. While many whites listen to and loath Farrakhan, for the reasons stated above, many African Americans appreciate his outspokenness against white supremacy and the expression of his love for black people, and the need for black people to love one another—a stance that also accounted for Malcolm X's great popularity from even those who ignored his advocacy of The Nation's brand of Islam. When the popular rap group, Public Enemy, took up these same themes of white supremacist critique and black-for-black love, in the late1980s and 1990s, some of its members embraced The Nation and were embraced by it. This alliance helped give race-consciousness rap a linkage with race-conscious religiosity. For a moment, hip-hop culture was both religious, and "black and proud."

The Nation of Islam exists in three splinter groups, (Minister Farrakhan's Nation, the five percent Nation of Islam and another breakaway faction, also called The Nation of Islam, on the east coast.) Estimates of the membership of all three range from 20,000-40,000.

The son of the Honorable Elijah Muhammad, founder of the NOI, is Wallace (changed to Wraith) Dean Muhammad.

Suspended for unorthodoxy, three times from The Nation during his father's lifetime, W. D. Muhammad led many of his followers into orthodox Sunni Islam after he became The Nation's head upon the death of his father in 1975. His followers comprise 200,000 of the estimated 500,000 to 1.5 million African-American Muslims in the United States. Another 17 or 18 different Muslim subgroups exist in the U.S.

What attracts adherents to the Islamic faith? Among the many reasons young adults give are: the revelation of the mercy and beneficence of Allah found in the Koran; the emphasis on the brotherhood of humanity, and the discipline of daily prayer and seasonal fasting in Ramadan. Islam's numbers within the black American community are fueled by one of three streams.

The first is a dissatisfaction with Christianity explained by criticisms both old and new, namely, that Christianity is viewed as a white religion, Christian churches are looked upon as being financially corrupt and ministers are seen as morally unfit. A second stream is from former Nation members who follow W.D. Muhammad. The third stream of converts comes from young adults searching for a coherent spiritual foundation. Most persons go through many different stages of religious belief and many go through many different religions in their lifetimes. For many of these, the clarity of the Koran, and the devotion of practicing, faithful Muslims help make Islam their final religious refuge.

African-American Muslims come from all classes, in all areas of this country. Islam in America can also boast of its "mega mosques" such as the 2, 000 member masjid (mosque) in Atlanta. In 1958, one scholar stated, that on a worldwide basis, where Christianity and Islam compete for converts, Islam was winning at a rate of ten to one. Such a growth rate might one day be replicated in the United States.

The Lesser Lights

Space does not allow a discussion of all of the religions black young adults are choosing. Among the most numerically significant are the the estimated 20,000 African-American Buddhists in the United States and the veneration of ancestors in the Ifa religion of the Yoruba faith. Another trend to note is the rise of African-American Gay and Lesbian liberation theology and the subsequent increase of the black inclusive churches, comprised of gay and lesbian African-American members.

Issues and Prospects

The fate and fortune of religion's relationship to black young adults, hinges on three questions underlying this entire article.

First, how will African-American religions fare in the competition with other worldviews such as the authority of science, relativism, humanism and pluralism? For example. Western science still argues that "man" (exclusive language intended here,) arrives at truth through the scientific method: observation, calculation, experimentation, hypothesizing, researching. This idea runs counter to what is at the heart of religion: spirit, inwardness, dependence, terrified and attracted awe of the divine, human connectedness and revelation. Issues such as the idea of cloning humans, altering human genetic structures, and the possibility of artificial intelligence assuming a life of its own, only complicate the question.

Second, how will gender and class issues affect religion? Black men between the ages of 25 and 35 are largely absent from most Christian churches. But while the Nation of Islam and mainstream Islam do better proportionally here, the majority of young Black men are absent even there, and from most of organized religion as well. Will religions reach out to male nonbelievers or will religionists have a "let them go to hell attitude."

Specialized men's ministries abound, while at the same time, there is an all female denomination in Los Angeles that has developed a mythical sister for Jesus Christ, Jessie Mae Christ, an African American goddess who is the essence of feminine spirituality. Outside of the Yoruba religion, black women still encounter gender oppression in most religions. A big question is whether patriarchal religions can challenge their own sexism and embrace women more fully.

In their text, *The Black Church in the African American Experience*, C. Eric Lincoln and Lawrence H. Mamiya warn that the black church is in danger of being divided into a two-tiered church—the middle-class church and the poorer black church. The growing black middle class, for the most part, no longer lives with, works with, socializes with, or even worships with the black underclass. At stake in contemporary black religion is whether black middle-class religious institutions can continue their historical trans-class, religious mission of *helping* to lift members of lower socioeconomic groups out of the grind of poverty.

Another issue to consider is the possible emergence of a prophetic wing in African-American religion that will grapple with economic, legal, political and social justice questions. Religious institutions can come to grips with the root causes of social problems or turn away from *changing* the society because of interpretations of the world based on their religious cosmology. As "compassionate conservatism" and "faith-based" opportunities arise, black religious groups of differing faiths can stop focusing on government *policies* and instead concentrate on their own separate *practices*.

A fundamental question is whether the former opportunities are genuinely new approaches or merely an attempt by those in power to build an "indebted constituency" of black (and other) religious leaders whose *appearance* seems to suggest the commitment of the federal government to black interests? Is there going to be a strong segment of the black church movement that can challenge white supremacist thought and practice, the misdistribution of wealth, and the gender oppressions of the dominant systems of the status quo?

Can religious groups come together within their religions and across their religions to address the multitude of needs of all Black Americans? If there is such a prophetic wing, will its strength stem from a narrowing of its religious focus or from a broad-minded understanding of this thing we call "reality."

These questions remind me of a scripture from the Bible, "it doth not yet appear... what we shall be..."

The Roots of Rap Music and Hip Hop Culture: One Perspective

BY YVONNE BYNOE

"Music is time, played live, played at seventy-eight rpms, thirty-three and a third, backwards, looped whatever. There's no translation. You understand or you don't."

From the novel, *White Boy Shuffle*, by Paul Beatty

Today even the most casual observer of popular culture has heard of rap music or hip hop, yet few can talk about either intelligibly. What is most significant to know is that rap music and hip-hop culture are American cultural expressions with their roots in the African Diaspora; they are part of a continuum steeped in the experiences of blacks in America. Moreover, despite the political insights that rap music often presents, it is not inherently political, radical or revolutionary. This music along with its associated hip-hop culture were developed as a source of entertainment for poor and working class black and Latino youth in New York City. The paradox of rap music is that it often alerts the public to problems concerning black Americans, however the values and behaviors that are frequently promoted in rap lyrics and hip-hop culture may actually exacerbate these issues.

The often-regurgitated story of rap music declares that it began in the early 1970s as the by-product of the desolate wasteland that was the South Bronx. In reality the seeds for rap music and the ethos of hip-hop culture were planted during the late 1960s in the aftermath of the assassinations of Martin Luther King, Jr. and Malcolm X and in the debris of decaying American cities, which finally exploded into the riots of 1966-1968. Despite hopes that federal civil rights legislation would facilitate racial equality, the Kerner Commission, appointed by President Johnson in 1967 to study the "urban problem" concluded that "America was moving toward two societies, one black and the other white" and that white racism was the principle cause of the 1967 disturbances.[i] Rather than rebuild devastated black communities or provide incentives for businesses to return, the government offered fleeting anti-poverty schemes. In addition to government divestment in its cities, the influx of heroin into urban communities and a national recession further ravaged an already vulnerable Black America; the South Bronx represented just one war torn region.

In the late 1960s and in the early 1970s, right before the advent of rap music, traditional R&B/soul artists realized that it was no longer enough for them to simply be singers. A select group of musical artists used their popularity and public platforms to be voices of change. In 1969 the Godfather of Soul, James Brown, joined the new black consciousness with "Say It Loud—I'm Black and I'm Proud" and Curtis Mayfield and the Impressions shifted from love songs to message songs like, "We're a Winner," "Choices of Colors" and "Check Your Mind." Crooner Marvin Gaye to the chagrin of Motown boss Berry Gordy in 1971 released the album, "What's Going On" that detailed ghetto life and the destruction of the Vietnam war and in 1973 Stevie Wonder's "Living for the City" became the first major hit to include a political message and samples of street sound (i.e., business, traffic, and voices).

The Last Poets pioneered street poetry, hard beats and scathing social criticism and in years to come would be known as the forefathers of hip hop. On May 19, 1968, these young poets came to Mount Morris Park in Harlem to commemorate Malcolm X's birthday. As these young men stood on stage accompanied by a drumbeat, they goaded the crowd to act with their chant, "Are you ready niggas," "You got to get ready." The work of The Last Poets predates the start of the controversy surrounding rap artists use of the word "nigga" (N-word) by nearly twenty years. In 1970, The Last Poets released their eponymous debut album and introduced the masterpiece, "Niggas are Scared of Revolution," a seething indictment on black apathy and mental slavery. Peter Bailey, a reporter with *The New York Times* said, *"They used the same techniques—*[used] *repetition, parable, testifying, signifying—that all great orators, preachers and soul singers so when they are trying to reach out and move the crowd..."* [ii] The proto-rap album (i.e., words rapped over music) is "Hustler's Convention" (1973) a cautionary tale about the dangers of street life, recorded by Last Poet member, Jalal Nurridi aka Lightnin' Rod. The Last Poets took their inspiration from Black Arts Movement poets, musicians such as John Coltrane and Sun Ra, and political and religious organizations like the Black Panthers and The Nation of Islam. Rap music and hip-hop culture thus emerged out of a mélange of government neglect, deferred American dreams, black nationalism and the genius of black youth. In the house parties, public parks, housing projects and local jams of New York City, poor and working-class black and Latino youth, developed their own world with its own laws.

While there are no definitive reports indicating the composition of the hip-hop community, it is safe to say that commercial radio and cable television helped to broaden the rap music fan base. The original rap music audience was primarily poor and working-class black and Latino teenagers from New York City. Today, anecdotal accounts portray the hip-hop community as multiracial and multi-generational, ranging in age from 12 to 40.[iii] Additionally, both young men and young women identify with hip hop. Economically, the rap fan is no longer necessarily poor or working class, although rap artists overwhelming still come from these backgrounds. Middle- and upper-middle-class black

Americans however are less likely than their white peers to identify with hip hop. This group generally supports the "spoken word" or poetry movement, which many view as more intellectual and "positive" than rap music and hip-hop culture. Ironically there is a rift within the spoken word movement regarding its relationship to hip hop; some spoken word artists openly embrace hip hop as their aesthetic foundation, while other young black poets are loath to call themselves part of the hip-hop community.

After the end of the of the Black Power Movement, the Vietnam War, and the FBI COINTELFO program, gangs were almost alone as the one institution in black inner-city communities offering a cogent message to black youth, "join and survive." The largest of these New York gangs was The Black Spades from the Bronx and its youthful leader Kevin Donovan, later renamed Afrika Bambattaa, and would transform The Black Spades into the Zulu Nation. Afrika Bambattaa was the name of a famous 19th-century Zulu chief, meaning Affectionate Leader. According to Bambattaa the gang life provided valuable lessons about how to deal with the system,

"To me the gangs were educational ... The Black Spades had unity among each other. The gang was like your family ....A lot of times when there were no jobs for youth, no trips happening in the community centres, the gangs got them [the government] there. If the gangs, 'scuse the expression, tore up shit, the government would start sending people to speak to you, throwing money to calm the gangs down. America is raised on violence. Only time America really listens is when somebody starts getting violent back." (Toop 57-58).

According to Zulu Nation records, Bambattaa founded the Zulu Nation on November 12, 1973 [iv] with the intent of establishing an organization that would aid in substituting gang fights and violence with rap, dance, and art. Hip-Hop culture therefore is comprised of four elements: Djing, MC'ing (rapping), Graffiti (aerosol art) and B-boying (breakdancing). Street gangs would become rap crews and battles for lyrical supremacy would replace actual street combat.

Cross-town from Bambattaa, Kool Herc aka Clive Campbell who had emigrated from Kingston, Jamaica in 1967 would introduce the concept of sound systems (massive speaker arrangements) and become recognized as the first hip-hop DJ. Kool Herc used simple toasts or raps to get the crowd moving while he mixed break beats between two turntables. A "break beat " is a thirty second break in the music where drums, bass and rhythm guitar are stripped down to their bare essence. Since mixing break beats required intense concentration Herc became the first DJ to use a dance team, comprised of B-boys (i.e., break boys; later called "breakdancers" by the media) to keep the party going as he worked the turntables.

Hip Hop originally began as an intellectual movement dominated by DJs like Grandmaster Flash and the Furious Five— audiophiles who collected records and searched all musical genres for new beats and samples; these young men were also technical wizards. Grandmaster Flash innovated "scratching" and learned how to "extend" music by playing two copies of the same record on two turntables. These and other techniques like "sampling" allowed DJs to signify on the messages of recorded music or to create entirely new music from the records. In this youth culture, the lyricists or MCs played a supporting role as ghetto philosophers, telling tales of life, fortune and love. The graffiti artists provided the visual backdrop for hip hop's evolution. Allegiance to hip hop as a community concept was never dependent on an association with a particular crew, but reflected a unity premised on hip hop's cultural aspects. In its early days, this street culture was almost exclusively black and thus this commonality encouraged young, gifted and black hip-hop performers to assert the fundamental elements of black cultural identity that had infused their upbringings.

Hip Hop culture, by its founding principles is inclusive, however despite attempts at revisionist history, white youth as a group were not early adopters of rap music. By the time the Sugar Hill Gang's "Rapper's Delight" hit the radio airwaves in 1979, rap music and hip-hop culture had been thriving underneath the commercial radar for almost a decade. Furthermore, most white people would still not hear about rap music until 1980 when punk rocker, Debbie Harry raps brief odes to Fab 5 Freddy and Grandmaster Flash's on Blondie's single "Rapture" (AutoAmerican). Six years later the success of The Beastie Boys, three upper-middle-class white boys from New York City, helped to expose the genre to white suburban youth. The bratty, prankster quality of the group and their music vaulted their debut album, "Licensed to Ill" (1986) into platinum selling status. In 1988, 15 years after the founding of Zulu Nation, "Yo' MTV Raps," a weekly show hosted by Hip Hop impresario, Fab 5 Freddy debuted and introduced rap music to a national audience. Surprisingly, many white kids wanted to be down with rap music, helping to make "Yo' MTV Raps" MTV's most successful show.

According to Soundscan, a computerized sales tracking system used by middle-to-large record retailers, 71 percent[v] of rap music consumers in America today are white and approximately 29 percent are black and Latino. The importance of Soundscan is that the music industry heavily relies on it to analyze the success of individual releases as well as individual musical genres. Soundscan figures are therefore integral to how rap music is marketed and to whom. Unfortunately, Soundscan is not an accurate method to gauge the buying capacity and tastes of black and Latino rap fans. Soundscan's numbers exclude record purchases made at "mom and pop" record stores that cannot afford to install the Soundscan system. These small stores often service black and Latino communities. Additionally, Soundscan does not account for the cheaper illegal or "bootleg" CDs that are purchased on the streets usually at a cost one-third the price of the legally authorized CDs. If these excluded rap music sales could be captured, an accurate report could show that black and Latino rap music fans purchase the same amount of rap music, if not more than white consumers. Also such a report may show that black and Latinos favor different rap artists than their white peers.

For the millions of white youth who have grown up on rap music, it represents the flagrant disregard for authority and social norms that they no longer find in rock and roll. According Dave Mays, a former rap radio DJ and head of The Source Entertainment, Inc. *"Hip Hop is the voice of a generation, just like rock n' roll was the voice of another generation. It speaks in an honest way. Kids identify with that."* (Hedges). Ironically, despite the considerable number of white rap music enthusiasts, the music has not substantively changed. White rap-rock hybrid groups like Limp Bizkit, Korn and Insane Clown Posse, have had some measure of success; however, whites are still drawn to rap music made by black artists. As Norman Mailer posits in his essay the "The White Negro," white teenagers seem to be attracted to rap music because black people still represent "the other," the hip, the exotic, the primitive. Thus if rap music and hip hop became more "white" it is conceivable that it would lose its appeal to white fans. The success of white rap artist Eminem therefore should be seen in perspective. In nearly thirty years of rap music history, there have only been four successful white acts, Vanilla Ice, The Beastie Boys, Third Base and now Eminem. Eminem however is different from his white predecessors in that he tells his story, that of a poor, white boy from Detroit, rather than simply aping or spoofing black rap artists. Given white fans proclivity to see black rap artists as the main agents of hip-hop culture, it is unlikely that Enimen's success will be replicated any time soon.

Although black talent and black interpretations of American life still dominate hip-hop culture in the media, black rap fans are increasingly finding themselves marginalized in the public dialogue of who and what constitutes hip hop. Currently, Eminem is the country's best selling rap artist, with over 8 million domestic sales of his sophomore album, The Marshall Mathers LP (2000). Eminem understandably is receiving international media attention but unlike black rap artists, he is also receiving accolades for his controversial lyrics. The nation's best selling and best known rap publication is *The Source* magazine, which is run by Dave Mays, a white man from Harvard University who co-founded it in 1989. *The Source* magazine has a circulation of 449,000 monthly and last year had gross revenues of $30 million dollars. In New York City, the number one media market in America, the Program Director for Hot 97, "The Home of Hip Hop and R&B" is Tracy Cloherty, a white woman. Lastly, at rap music concerts white fans are steadily becoming the majority of the audiences since high-ticket prices and the venue locations exclude many less affluent black fans. Not only have fifty- and sixty-dollar rap concert tickets become the norm, increasingly rap concerts are not held in cities, but in suburban stadiums like The Continental Airlines Arena in New Jersey that require that concert goers drive to the event. Therefore, the need to have a car prohibits many black and Latino youth from attending these rap concerts even if they are able to afford to purchase a ticket.

The issue of rap music and hip-hop culture is not black and white *per se* but whether or not hip-hop culture can really be egalitarian in a society still plagued by racial discrimination. In essence, if whites by and large are the hip-hop industry's[vi] owners and gatekeepers and blacks are primarily hired talent, does this configuration constitute new racial harmony or is it simply an updated version of the same power structure? The concerns of black and Latino youth remain different from those of white youth if for no other reason than because of intractability of racial discrimination, which often results in economic inequity. In 1996 the typical black household had a net worth of $4,500, one-tenth that of the average white household; poverty among black children is at 40 percent; and according to 1995 figures young black males are murdered at the startling rate of 111 per 100,000. Young black men also are more likely than young white men to be victims of police brutality. Most recently Cincinnati, Ohio erupted with protests and vandalism after police killed an unarmed black man. The 19 year old was the fifteenth person shot by police since 1995 and the fourth shot since November.

The chief issue is whether hip hop, which now aggressively targets white fans, can simultaneously represent the interests of poor and working-class black and Latino youth.

From the perspective of the music industry, white rap fans are a sizable market to be exploited financially, thus in the past decade or so, the relevant rap music customer has morphed from black youth in the cities into white youth in the suburbs. Thus rather than providing a wide range of rap messages to be heard and shared cross-culturally, the music industry has instead fixated on renegade black rap artists who epitomize the anti-social behavior preferred by rebellious white youth. Thus despite the existence of "conscious" rap artists like Common and Mos Def or political rap artists like dead prez, who discuss the empowerment of the black community, the music industry tends to more heavily promote artists like Jay-Z or Sean "Puffy" Combs who celebrate individualism, lavish lifestyles, promiscuity and criminality. This limited view of black youth, rather than inspiring hip hop to be progressive or educational is actually reactionary, reinforcing old stereotypes.

If whites now control the direction and tone of rap music and hip-hop culture, then middle-class black record executives and entrepreneurs assisted in the takeover. As young whites began exploring rap music in the early 1980s, young middle-class black Americans, shunned the ghetto-derived music, in favor of upscale disco music. One important example is Frankie Crocker, the former program director for WBLS-FM, then regarded as the premiere black radio station in the nation. Crocker was an early cheerleader for disco music and thus chose not to include rap music on the station's play list. Moreover, in 1977 WBLS-FM changed its tag line from, "the total black experience in sound" to "the total experience in sound" signaling an important program shift from black funk and soul music to "colorless" disco music. As expected, other black music and radio executives followed WBLS' lead and totally ignored rap music.

The few blacks who entered the rap music business in its early days were music industry veterans with limited business experience. Early black-owned record companies like Sugar Hill Records, Winley Records and Enjoy Records were small-scale operations. Management and financial problems coupled with these companies' reluctance to hire younger talent scouts made them less able to capitalize on the new rap genre. It is notable that historically white-owned record companies like Chess Records and Stax produced black music primarily because they saw it as an economic opportunity; love of the music often was a secondary consideration. By contrast, when the original black-owned rap record companies faded, black entrepreneurs (young and old) with business savvy and/or access to capital did not attempt to replace them, even as a quick money making opportunity.

The lack of interest in rap music, even as a business venture, by the black middle class allowed young, college educated, white entrepreneurs the chance to enter the world of hip hop as record company owners.[vii] The only middle-class black person to be part of this group was Russell Simmons who began the Def Jam empire with Rick Rubin in 1977. These white-owned, independent rap record companies were followed into the marketplace by multinational conglomerates with global distribution capabilities. The multinationals either formed partnerships with these white-owned independent rap record companies and/or established their own internal rap music divisions.

Today, with a few exceptions like Master P's independently owned, No Limit Records, the majority of black rap record labels contractually are dependent subsidiaries of larger corporations. These rap record label relationships range from production deals which essentially pay rap producers set fees to find and package talent to joint ventures like Bad Boy Entertainment (Arista) and Roc-a-Fella Records (Def Jam/Universal) where the label and the parent company agree to share proportionally in overhead expenses, the profits and the losses associated with the rap record label. What is clear is that while many black rap artists/record executives brag about their record labels, usually it is white executives who own the record and media companies who ultimately determine what rap music is produced and broadcast globally. The business owners therefore control hip hop.

According to The Reverend Osagyefo Uhuru Sekou, "*[r]ap is a melodic commentary about God, gangstas, poverty, wealth, ethos, sexist values, racist systems, emotional status, varied contexts, contemporary history, and real and mythical insights on reason for being. It encompasses an urban daze of (sur)real stories of soul searching on city streets.*" (*UrbanSouls, pp.* 110-111). However, one of the chief concerns within and without the hip-hop community is the gratuitous use of profanity and the N-word, as well as lyrics that denigrate women. In October of last year, the National Action Network and The Source Entertainment convened a summit to address social responsibility in hip hop. More recently, rap artists KRS-One and Chuck D publicly joined Minister Conrad Muhammad's challenge to music industry executives and artists to change the tone of rap music. While profanity and the careless use of the N-word are disturbing, often this language merely mirrors that real life language of these artists. The coarsening of American popular culture has encouraged this incivility under the guise of "free speech." More troubling however is the use of terms like "bitches" and "ho's" to describe black women. Occasionally, rap artists attempt to defend their language by stating that bitches and 'ho's are only those women who use sex to get money from men. Nevertheless, many rappers indiscriminately use these words, such that they are virtual synonyms for "women." Rap music represents a far deeper misogyny in the black community, as well as in the white male community that buys and listens to rap. Concerned citizens can change the direction of rap music by organizing efforts that make the production and broadcast of objectionable material cease being profitable for record companies, radios and cable television stations.

Many within the hip-hop generation have come to believe that this country's leadership has used rap music as a scapegoat to avoid doing the hard work of actually changing the circumstances of poor and working class black people in this country. Prophetic leadership understands that in order to change the messages of rap music and hip-hop culture, the circumstances from which they spring must first be changed. This means working with the hip-hop community to bring back a semblance of dignity and humanity to the 'hoods, wards and barrios of America in the form of substantially improved schools, healthcare, employment opportunities, housing, childcare and counseling services. Rap music and hip-hop culture can be agents of change if people are willing to look beyond its hard façade inelegant language and corporate co-option in order to fully examine what really needs to be so that no child is left behind.

References

Blondie. *AutoAmerican*. Chrysalis, 1980.

Eminem. *The Marshall Mathers LP.* Interscope, 2000.

Grandmaster Flash and the Furious Five. *The Message (12" single)*.

Sugar Hill Records, 1982.

Hedges, Chris. "Magazine Succeeds As Hip-Hop Source." *Tampa Tribune Newspaper Online*. 23 February 2001 <http://www.tampatrib.com/baylifenews/MGA0IJSKKJC.htm>.

Muwakkil, Salim. "From An Activist's Standpoint." *Chicago Tribune Newspaper Online*. 9 April 2001. <http://www.Chicagotribune.com/news/opinion/commentary/article/0,2669, SAV-0104090025, FF.html>.

Sekou, Osagyefo Uhuru. *UrbanSouls*. St. Louis: Urban Press, 2001.

The Beastie Boys. *Licensed to Ill*. Def Jam Recordings, 1986.

Toop, David. *Rap Attack 2 African Rap to Global Hip Hop*. London: Serpent's Tail, 1991.

[i] Report of the National Advisory Commission on Civil Disorders released on March 1, 1968, later known as the Kerner Commission Report.

[ii] Quote taken from article (title unknown) that appeared in the May 31, 1970 edition of the newspaper.

[iii] Several years ago the maximum age for the Hip Hop community was thought to be 35, however that maximum continues to creep upward. Some of the leading voices of Hip Hop culture like Chuck D, KRS-One, are nearing 40 years old; Russell Simmons is over 40 years old. Moreover, Min. Conrad Muhammad, known as the Hip Hop Minister, who has been involved in a public debate with Russell Simmons over the direction of Hip Hop is 36 years old.

[iv] See <http://www.Zulunation.com/history>.

[v] Soundscan statistics cited in the article, "Black Like Them" by Charles Aaron that appeared in the November, 1998 issue of *Spin* magazine. Incidentally, The Recording Industry Association of America (RIAA) in the same year indicated the percentage of white rap buyers at 60 percent, showing the variance in statistics.

[vi] The hip-hop industry as used in this discussion consists of the business concerns i.e. record companies, music video shows, commercial radio stations, press, fashion/style entities contracted rap artists and producers. The hip-hop community is distinguished from the hip-hop community which is comprised of fans often initiate trends and who legitimize artists through record sales or by giving artists critical acclaim aka "street credibility."

[vii] Examples include: Tommy Silverman (Tommy Boy Records); Corey Robbins (Profile Records); Aaron Fuchs (Tuff City Records).

Their Characteristic Music: Thoughts on Rap Music and Hip Hop Culture

BY DAVID W. BROWN

Almost four decades ago, Amiri Baraka declared that African-American music was inextricably linked to African-American history; in fact, according to Baraka, the music *was* the history. In his groundbreaking and influential book *Blues People: Negro Music in White America*, he stated that throughout American history, "[a]t each juncture, twist, and turn, as black people were transformed, so was their characteristic music." Baraka applied this trenchant cultural critique to slave work songs, spirituals, blues, and jazz, demonstrating that black social and economic development was reflected in the music, and that the music had a profound influence on white America as well. Baraka's insight about the past applies to the present as well: We must examine hip-hop music to understand the under-35 generation of African Americans. The music reflects the environment, artistry, ambitions, fears, and possibilities of young black people. It also sheds light on some of the enduring incongruities of American race relations.

Rap music burst onto the national scene in the late 1970s, and has withstood nearly two decades of predictions of its imminent demise. Instead, rap and hip hop have soared. Last year its sales accounted for 12.9 percent of the $14.3 billion national music market, making it second in popularity only to the 25-percent share held by rock music.

Rap has spawned hip-hop culture—an attitude, a *pose*, and a way of behaving that has deeply influenced music videos, movies, fashion, technology, advertising, and sports. This essay explores some of the more unambiguously positive aspects of hip hop, focusing on developments in the past decade. For example, hip hop is a testament to the resourcefulness and inventiveness of the post-civil rights era generation. Hip hop also demonstrates the continuing tendency among black people toward self-reinvention; some of the most discerning social commentary from young black people is expressed in rap lyrics. Moreover, hip hop's increasing growth and mainstream popularity show that black youth are maintaining an old tradition: they are again America's music and cultural vanguard.

Nonetheless, some aspects of hip-hop culture have always been troubling, and remain so. The reason is that rap reflects some of the most serious dilemmas facing these young African Americans—such as the staggering incarceration of young black men (and, increasingly, women), the persistent lack of meaningful opportunity, and the casual veneration of violence, misogyny, and other forms of social pathology. The "gangsta" facet of rap music seems to be self-consciously following Baraka's suggestion that "[e]ach response a man makes to his environment helps make a more complete picture of him, no matter what that response is."

That's one reason hip hop is also a fault line that divides African Americans of different ages; it is keenly disparaged by many blacks over 35. Yet, an extraordinary dimension of rap music and hip-hop culture is that the most insightful and effective commentary can be found within the genre itself.

Since its foundation is in beats and rhymes, rap music has grown in infinite directions, making it impossible to generalize about the genre. Some rappers, like Slick Rick, are colorful storytellers who are prone to employ a narrative structure. One of the most common motifs is for rappers to issue an incessant series of boasts about their lyrical skills, sex appeal, or affluence. Some bohemian rappers favor sly, intellectual lyrics; others tap into the theology of The Nation of Islam or mysticism of the Five Percent Nation. Although rap has produced numerous pop superstars (think MC Hammer or Will Smith) who concoct danceable, radio-friendly hits, other artists (Public Enemy, for instance) deliver a blistering and uncompromising political message. One of rap's most commercially successful, and controversial, subgenres has been dubbed "gangsta rap." This term is of limited utility because to a large extent it is a media-imposed label that is branded on pretty much every rap album that features explicit lyrics, whether or not the music depicts the criminal hedonism that is gangsta rap's hallmark. At its worst, gangsta rap celebrates America's worst nightmare: criminally minded, young black men with a penchant for violence, vulgarity, and vice. In the early 1990s, gangsta rappers such as Ice-T and Snoop Doggy Dogg, who hailed from Los Angeles, helped to break New York City's overwhelming influence on rap music. Rappers with unique regional styles continue to achieve national success, from Outkast (Atlanta) to Master P and Juvenile (New Orleans) to Nelly (St. Louis). Additionally, from Salt-N-Pepa to Missy Elliott, women have expanded the musical boundaries of rap music and provided a more assertive role model than the traditional female pop star.

Rap music burgeoned into hip-hop culture as its infectious spirit revitalized and transformed other (sometimes moribund) aspects of art, commerce, and society. Hip hop's influence on other forms of music cannot be underestimated. During the late 1980s, producers like Teddy Riley breathed new life into rhythm and blues by steeping it in hip hop to create a sound called "new jack swing." Today, most R&B artists can also be considered part of hip hop; Mary J. Blige and Destiny's Child are examples. Even the teeny-bopper R&B music popularized by white "boy bands" like the Backstreet Boys is derivative of hip hop. By the mid-1990s, gospel singers like Kirk Franklin began to embrace hip hop, contributing to an explosion in gospel's popularity. And recently, after several false starts, the fusion of rock and hip hop seems to be firmly established as a pop music fixture. The generation of white youth who grew up listening to rap has little use for fixed divisions between disparate genres, and acts such as Limp Bizkit and Kid Rock have ridden this trend to the top of the charts.

A new generation of black entrepreneurs has capitalized on hip hop, too. Most of these businessmen, like Russell Simmons and Sean "Puff Daddy" Combs, built their fortunes by partnering with a major label. For example, Combs' Bad Boy label is part of BMG Entertainment. However, an alternative business model exists: Percy Miller, better known as Master P, built a hugely successful independent recording company called No Limit, relying on a major label only for distribution and pocketing tremendous profits. In 1999, at age 29, he was number 28 on *Fortune* magazine's "40 Richest Under 40" list, with an estimated net worth of $361 million. And each of these entrepreneurs has built their label into an empire that markets a variety of other products, such as movies, clothing, and toys; Simmons has even begun to dabble in politics.

According to music critic Nelson George, the "molding of technology to fit a black aesthetic became a hallmark of hip hop." Some of hip hop's technological developments stem from using existing technology in new ways. For example, old school DJs found countless ways to utilize the combination of two turntables. Rappers and producers were also quick to exploit the potential of new electronic equipment, such as the drum machine. One of hip hop's most influential breakthroughs is "sampling." This technique involves using a digital device called a sampler to capture a portion of an existing musical recording—from a two-second snare drum fragment to a fraction of a Coltrane solo to the entire chorus of a soul classic—which is then looped repeatedly in the creation of a new song.

The sampling explosion that occurred in the late 1980s shook the music industry in many ways. The courts established that a song could not be sampled without its owner's permission, requiring musicians to purchase the rights to the works they wanted to sample, often for exorbitant prices. This precedent dramatically increased the values of the back catalogs of many musicians, especially funk, soul, and disco acts, which hip-hop artists sought for thumping basslines or catchy vocal hooks. Although some critics complain that reusing a portion of another song demonstrates a lack of creativity, sampling has become a common aspect of songcraft across many musical genres.

Since its inception, hip-hop culture has been associated with distinctive style trends, such as Adidas sneakers and thick gold chains in the '80s and oversized jeans and rugged work boots in the 1990s. Established brands, such as Polo and Tommy Hilfiger, have cashed in by redesigning their clothing lines to fit the tastes of the hip-hop generation. Black designers and entrepreneurs have also recognized the potential of this market, leading to the creation of such companies as Phat Farm, Sean John, and FUBU, which is an acronym for "For Us, By Us."

In short, the hip-hop aesthetic continues to color American culture in myriad ways. It crops up in the latest popular slang phrases, dance moves, and expressive gestures, such as the cocky swagger of a corn-rowed basketball player in baggy shorts after a rim-rattling slam dunk. Rap music now sells everything from McDonalds and Coca-Cola to the latest summer blockbuster. Thus, hip-hop style is indelibly branded on America and present and powerful around the globe—from Paris to Johannesburg to Tokyo.

Hip hop music is consistent with many aspects of the African-American cultural tradition. For example, like many other black artistic developments, hip hop can be considered heroically inventive, a way to transcend the hopelessness and despair of life in America's inner cities. As hip-hop critic Kevin Powell explains, "hip-hop is urban folk art, and as much an indication of the conditions in impoverished areas as bluesman Robert Johnson's laments in the 1930s.

Hip hop was the innovation of black youth who did not have the resources to assemble a band that used expensive instruments. Instead, all its pioneers needed were two turntables, a microphone, a crate of old records, and the rhyming skills to make a crowd throw its hands in the air and scream.

Rappers' intricate rhyme schemes, creative metaphors, clever allusions, and verbal dexterity showcase the ingenuity of young African Americans and their "kinetic orality," as Harvard professor Cornel West has put it. And hip hop underscores the African-American affinity for self-reinvention: grandiose nicknames, stage names, and alter egos are prevalent in hip hop. For example, rap star Christopher Wallace was better known under the monikers of the Notorious B.I.G. and Biggie Smalls.

Hip hop is not only an extension of black heritage; it also reflects the unique characteristics of the under-35 generation, and the way that America as a whole is changing. More than any other black musical development, hip hop is part of mainstream culture. For example, the white youth culture of the 1960s was largely driven by rock and roll (although by the middle of the decade the urbanized soul music of the Motown machine—with its bold declaration that it was "The Sound of Young America" was exerting significant influence as well), which was derivative of the lesser-known Delta blues. But in contemporary America, white youth experience hip hop directly. A *Newsweek* poll of last fall confirms the hip hop's popularity among a wide cross-section of young people—three quarters of all voters under 30 say they listen to rap at least occasionally.

That crossover appeal has been readily apparent since the mid-1980s, when Run-D.M.C. achieved pop success by collaborating with the rock band Aerosmith, and the Beastie Boys, three white rappers, released an album that sold over four million copies. Today, the musical mixing continues, most prominently in the collaborations between Dr. Dre, a rapper and producer who is the architect of the West Coast gangsta sound, and his protégé Eminem, a white rapper from Detroit who has sold more than 11 million albums and collected three awards at the 2001 Grammys. From Al Jolson through Elvis, the Beastie Boys, and now Eminem, White America has been fascinated by white musicians who perform black musical styles. A new twist for the current generation, however, is that Eminem is a white rapper who has found acclaim for his rhyming skills and flow not only in the suburbs but among black devotees of hip hop as well.

Even though hip hop was born in gritty inner-city neighborhoods such as Harlem and Compton, recently, it has begun to echo the rise of the black middle class and this demographic group's increasing visibility in American life. Hip hop music in the last decade, especially as produced by hit-maker Sean "Puff Daddy" Combs, was often stripped of its coarse and urgent ghetto aesthetic. Rap became increasingly prone to sample popular black music of the 1970s, casually evoking a pleasant nostalgia, while the lyrics included chatter about the trappings of prosperity, like Gucci clothes and Cristal champagne. In another example, R&B's embrace of hip hop and the increasing black exodus to the suburbs were conterminous: the black middle class was receptive to music that bounced to the hip-hop beat but left behind some of rap's dissonance.

However, hip hop also echoes some of the most serious social problems that black America faces. Three of the most disturbing trends in the music are its fetish for crime and violence, obsession with materialism, and degrading treatment of women; this article uses the imprecise term gangsta rap as a catchall phrase to describe music in thrall to these trends.

Gangsta rap recorded the crack epidemic that hit inner cities and the accompanying rise in inner-city gang warfare. It is often stripped of melody, instead employing stark beats that echo the danger and uncertainty of inner-city life. The lyrics express the nihilism of young black men who see a prison stint as a rite of passage, and an early, violent death as almost inevitable destiny. Although some rappers suggest that their work should be regarded as fiction, many have built their careers by maintaining that they truly are, or were, real criminals. Worse, these are not just consequence-free boasts; many rappers have been unable to escape violent crime. Tupac Shakur and the Notorious B.I.G., arguably the two most talented and charismatic rappers of their generation, were shot and killed in drive-by shootings in 1996 and 1997, respectively. Their murders remain unsolved, but their deaths are widely attributed to a feud between East Coast and West Coast rap labels. In December 1999, gunfire erupted near rap mogul Puff Daddy and his entourage in a New York nightclub. In March, Puffy's protégé Shyne was convicted of first-degree assault in connection with the shooting; he faces up to 25 years in prison.

Gangsta rap also expresses an obsessive devotion to materialism; some songs sound like a rhyming catalogue of high-end consumer goods. Rappers flaunt diamond-encrusted, or "iced down," rings, Rolexes, and platinum medallions—even mouths full of diamond-covered teeth. They glide through hedonistic music videos in ostentatious Bentley convertibles (worth nearly a quarter of a million dollars), gloating about owning mansions and name dropping designers from Versace to Dolce & Gabbana. From people who otherwise love to pose as beyond the boundary of staid, conventional society, this slavish, follow-the-steps attention to the details of haute-bourgeois consumerism, to acquiring the credentials of belonging, bespeak a *yearning* that is worthy of far more study.

All too often, rap lyrics encourage men to aspire to a lifestyle of pimping, and malign women as whores who will do anything for money. Rap videos are frequently consumed with blatant images of female objectification, such as parades of writhing, scantily clad dancers. And not only do gangsta rappers broadcast disturbing messages about crime, money, and misogyny—they do so through a haze of blunt smoke, while swilling booze and peppering their language with profanity.

But gangsta rap can be defended. Many gangsta rappers are simply expressing the circumstances in which they have been raised: It is useful to recall that Amiri Baraka characterized the be bop style of jazz as "willfully harsh and anti-assimilationist" music that was born out of black frustration with white America, and gangsta rap can be described similarly.

Furthermore, rappers are not only reflecting the values of the inner city; they are in tune with mainstream trends. Sex sells everywhere in America today, even in Pepsi commercials, and the unprecedented economic booms of, first, the 1980s', and then the 1990s' dot-com explosion fueled an extraordinary preoccupation with gaudiness throughout our society. Moreover, America has had a long fascination with outlaws, from Hollywood films like "The Public Enemy" and "The Godfather" to the current HBO hit series "The Sopranos." The creators of gangsta rap are shrewd businessmen—they know that their criminal braggadocio helps to sell millions of albums in the suburbs. And not surprisingly, the bitterness, raw anger, and rejection of middle-class values in this genre of music make it even more appealing to disaffected white youth.

Some of the criticism of hip hop can be attributed to a generation gap. American parents have often been shocked and offended by the music that their children listen to. Some of the most vocal critics of rap within the black community, such as C. Dolores Tucker and Rev. Calvin Butts, bring a civil-rights-era approach to their disapproval, noting that the vulgarity in the music is at odds with the visions of black heroes like Dr. Martin Luther King, Jr. In another example of the age gap, civil rights legend Rosa Parks has sued the rap duo Outkast for using her name as the title of one of their hit singles, because she does not want her name associated with a song that is laced with profanity. For their part, Outkast maintain that the eponymous title is a tribute to Rosa Parks.

Some of the criticism rap now receives is historically redundant. The blues, now venerated as folk art, were once widely derided as a vulgar, low-class music. Jazz, especially in its more experimental forms, such as bebop, was often scorned by mainstream music critics or dismissed as "beatnik" music. Rock musicians such as Elvis and the Rolling Stones were accused of corrupting the nation's youth by promoting promiscuity, drug abuse, and disrespect for authority.

These rationalizations for the increasing popularity of controversial hip-hop music can, however, be countered with justifiable concerns about the coarsening of American culture and the searing images and sounds of depravity to which impressionable children are exposed. The question how to address such concerns is difficult to answer, especially for a society that prizes First Amendment ideals such as free speech and freedom of expression, and celebrates the free market.

The urge to place warning labels on rap albums, restrict its sale or advertising, and heap moral opprobrium on the producers and distributors of the music is not new. It has periodically flared up since 1985, when Tipper Gore founded the Parents' Music Resource Center and testified in Congress about dirty lyrics. In the early 1990s, the 2 Live Crew obscenity trials occurred, and Warner Bros. faced boycotts when one of its subsidiaries released Ice-T's "Cop Killer" song. Today's particular bogeyman is Eminem, who by even gangsta rap standards has pushed boundaries (he has rapped about raping and killing his mother).

Government agencies and politicians have recently focused their attention on how violent music, movies, and video games are marketed to children. The Federal Trade Commission (FTC) has released reports stating that record companies frequently advertise gangsta rap albums to minors. For example, about 41 percent of viewers of a hip-hop show on Black Entertainment Television, *Top Ten Live at 106th & Park*, and about 44 percent of the readership of *Vibe*, a hip-hop magazine, are under 18 years old, and rap with explicit lyrics is frequently advertised in these media outlets. In response to this report, Sen. Joe Lieberman (D; Conn.), with Sen. Hillary Clinton (D; NY) as a co-sponsor, introduced the Media Marketing Accounting Act into the Senate. This bill would give the FTC the authority to prevent music with explicit content, which includes "strong language or expressions of violence, sex, or substance abuse" from being marketed to an "audience [that] is comprised of a substantial proportion of minors." The FTC would be able to impose civil fines on companies that violated the act.

Whether this law will be passed is uncertain, and whether it would survive a constitutional challenge seems even more dubious. But while politicians are fashioning heavy-handed, punitive approaches to gangsta rap, hip hop is developing its own creative response. After years of wandering in the gangsta wilderness, there are signs that hip hop is addressing more pressing topics than diamonds and guns.

Social commentary is a deep-rooted tradition in black music, as demonstrated by Billie Holiday's lament for lynching victims, "Strange Fruit." In the early 1970s, this tradition flourished with artists such as Marvin Gaye, Aretha Franklin, and Stevie Wonder, who championed black pride and condemned black-on-black violence. At the same time, some of the artists who helped create the blueprint for rap, such as Gil Scott-Heron and The Last Poets, were releasing albums that promoted an explicit revolutionary agenda. A little further along, "The Message," a 1982 hit song by Grandmaster Flash and the Furious Five, was a gritty tale of inner-city blues. In the late 1980s and early 1990s, Public Enemy was rap's authoritative conscience, speaking out on subjects like Reagan-era social policies, a national holiday for Dr. Martin Luther King, Jr., and drug and alcohol abuse.

Today, some of the best critique of the gangsta rap mentality of American social problems comes from more "conscious" hip-hop artists like Lauryn Hill, Wyclef Jean, Common, the Roots, and Mos Def. These artists have transcended the stale debate over whether hip hop is primarily a cause or mostly a reflection of problems like violence and sexism. Instead, they emphasize that these social dilemmas are obstacles to be overcome, and that the African-American tradition is rich with examples of high achievement. For example, Lauryn Hill has released singles that urge young women to avoid teenage pregnancy and encourage them to hang on to their self-esteem in the face of adversity. One of Common's themes is that rappers should respect the African-American tradition of music being used to uplift its listeners, an idea that is reflected in lyrics such as: "Music is a gift that is sacred/I opened it, used it/Hoping you can grow to it."

These artists also offer a direct critique of gangsta rap. Some of them, like Mos Def, have noted that the gangsta image is "minstrelsy because that's what white people want to believe about us—that it's about 'money, cash, hos' for all of us." Others warn that the gangsta lifestyle is likely to lead to self-destruction, or that the pursuit of spiritual enrichment is more rewarding than material gain. They condemn anti-intellectualism and laud the quest for knowledge and self-awareness. And by avoiding the temptation to get paid by using their talents to celebrate urban nihilism, these musicians are providing an example of personal integrity and social responsibility for their generation. They are demonstrating that it's possible to have a hit single that is positive without sounding preachy, that is profound and not profane. Together with the current resurgence of a more soulful, more conscious form of R&B, as evidenced by artists such as Erykah Badu, Macy Gray, and Musiq

Soulchild, hip hop's earnest backlash against gangsta rap is a good indication that some part of the under-35 generation is more community-oriented than its critics may realize. There will always be a market for gangsta rap, because what it expresses is as American as cherry pie. But the black musical tradition continues to reverberate with the moral resiliency and artistic creativity of the African-American spirit.

The New York Urban League Survey: Black New York—On Edge, But Optimistic

WALTER W. STAFFORD

In the waning decades of the 20th century, New York City was transformed from a magnet for U.S.- and Caribbean-born blacks to the center of the Diaspora of people of African descent. From Ethiopia to Panama, from Ghana to Brazil, immigrants of African descent streamed into the city's neighborhoods, enriching black culture with their languages and religions, and extending the range of black political interests. In 1996, more than one-fourth of the city's black population was foreign-born, primarily from the Caribbean. The 2000 census is expected to document a much higher proportion of foreign-born among the black population; they themselves were part of the massive surge of immigrants of color who came to the city in the last two decades. Of the top twenty source countries of immigrants to the city, only three—the former Soviet Union, Poland, and Yugoslavia—were European.

This new wave of immigrants of color, coupled with the out-migration white city residents has produced an historic "re-arrangement" of New York's population. Non-Hispanic whites are now 35 percent of the population; non-Hispanic blacks, 25 percent; and persons of Hispanic origin, 27 percent. While the city has historically been a port-of-entry for European immigrants, it has never received groups of color in such numbers, and this is the first time that whites have had to share proportional status.

The demographic transition—the most significant since the end of World War II is transforming New York City's black civil society, as well. Before World War II, Black New York had grown steadily but slowly. Between 1940-1950, however, 221,000 new black migrants, mainly from the Southern coastal states, arrived (Rosenwaike, 1972). The new migrants, who accounted for 76 percent of the black population growth, forced black institution—churches, and social and political organizations—to adjust their strategies of internal acculturation and external protest for equal education, jobs, and other resources. The current transformation is more complex because of the variety of those coming in—notably from Black Africa—and the out-migration of native-born blacks to the South. While the current adjustments are not immune from cultural and political tensions, the thread of historical oppression and contemporary discrimination has enveloped blacks from disparate places in a collective pathos if not a common agenda. It is of the greatest significance that their shared view of having to endure a collective unfairness draws blacks in a bond across incomes, occupations, and place of origin.

Concerned about the growing complexity of the black population, their problems, and their views about institutions in the city, the New York Urban League commissioned a random telephone survey of 801 black households in 2000. The survey was taken during an important transformation of the city's economy and social arrangements: As one of the major centers of global finance, New York City's economy flourished in the middle and late 1990s. However, the benefits to the residents have been uneven. The gap between the rich and the poor widened to the largest in any U.S. metropolitan area, and joblessness and poverty—especially among blacks and Latinos—remained stubbornly high.

The survey also came amidst a three-year period of heightened tension and discussion within the city over relations between blacks and New York's predominately white police force, relations that were a constant reminder of untended wounds. That was ironically fitting, because New York City began the 20th century with turmoil between blacks and white policemen. In 1900, Arthur Harris, a black man fatally stabbed an undercover white policeman in a scuffle after the officer claimed he had arrested his wife for soliciting. Harris disappeared, but thousands of "sympathizers" for the slain officer unleashed their fury on innocent blacks. Police often stood and watched or engaged in the melee (Johnson, 1972; Otley, 1943). The riot lasted for several days and left hundreds of blacks injured (Ovington, 1911). Nearly a century later, in 1997, Abner Louima's savage beating in a police station by white officers, and, two years later, Amadou Diallo's death at the hands of four white plainclothes officers (who, they claimed, mistook his wallet for a gun), for a time underscored the justifiable distrust most blacks have of the police. Significantly, both men were part of the new wave of black immigrants: Louima from Haiti, and Diallo from Guinea, West Africa.

Thus, the New York Urban League survey expresses blacks' views of racial discrimination in general and the police in particular at a critical moment in the city's history. Yet, the survey's importance is much broader, too, because it asked respondents to identify their economic and social needs, assess their life chances, and voice their opinions about a range of topics from the plight of young black males, to school vouchers, to their participation in religious and civic organizations.

Research and Organization of the Discussion

The backgrounds of the respondents reflected the demographic characteristics of the city. Forty-four percent were men and 56 percent were women. Fifty-five percent were born in the United States and 38 percent in New York City; 44 percent were born elsewhere in the African Diaspora. Only 26 percent had resided in the city for more than twenty-five years. Thirty-one percent were married, 17 percent were separated or divorced, and 39 percent had never been married. Twenty-one percent of the households reported family incomes of $50,000 or more, while 79 percent had incomes below that level. Twenty-six percent had completed four or more years of college, and one-third had completed high school.

The majority of the respondents were Protestant, but the remaining group, mirroring the new diversity of black civil society, included Buddhists, Muslims, and Rastafarians, among others. The political views of the respondents were balanced: 35 percent identified themselves as very to somewhat liberal; 32 percent said that they were somewhat or very conservative. Native-born blacks were much more liberal than those born in the Caribbean or Africa.

Only 3 percent of the blacks in the survey said they were self-employed, a rate close to that reported by the 1990 census. There was little difference in the responses of native and foreign-born blacks.

The findings of the survey are divided into two parts: (1) A discussion of the major problems identified by the respondents, and (2) family activity and community relations. In addition, the survey data are complemented by data from other sources, including the census and other government reports. Where possible and relevant the household income, place of origin, gender, and the educational status of the respondents are compared.

Major Problems Identified by Black New Yorkers

The respondents identified five major problems: (1) economic development, jobs and unemployment; (2) discrimination and racism; (3) police relations; (4) crime and violence; and (5) education. These five areas, which overlap, accounted for 66 percent of the problems identified by the respondents (Table 1).

Economic Development, Jobs and Unemployment

Blacks' focus on economic issues reflects their limited access to higher paying jobs, their high unemployment rates, and their lack of access to capital for business formation: 18.5 percent of those responding identified economic development and jobs as the leading problem: the proportion is higher if the 4 percent that identified job training are added; 53 percent indicated that the most important goal for black's as a community was increased economic opportunity.

Persistently high unemployment rates have plagued the black community in economic upturns and downturns. In 1999, for example, despite the economic boom, the unemployment rate for black men was 11.8 percent and the black female rate was 10.4 percent, compared to a citywide average of 6.7 percent. Almost unnoticed were the increasingly volatile unemployment rates of black women. In 1997, the unemployment rate for black women reached 15 percent, their highest rate since the late 1970s. Slightly more than one-fourth of the respondents (26 percent) reported that someone in their household had been unemployed in the past year and 23 percent were very concerned about losing their jobs. There were few differences by origin of birth, although foreign-born respondents indicated greater concern about losing their jobs.

The economic problems of the black households were magnified by their dependence on welfare. Over 90 percent of the recipients of the city's Temporary Assistance for Needy Families (TANF) are black or Latino. According to 1999 data, blacks were 40 percent of the TANF households. Fifteen percent of the respondents (19 percent of women) indicated that at least one or more persons in their household were on welfare in the last five years, including 40 percent of the respondents with incomes under $10,000.

Lack of income also influenced housing selection. Over half (54 percent) indicated that they would move if they could afford it. Respondents in lower-income households expressed slightly greater interest in moving.

Finally, income status affected access to health care and retirement planning. Nearly half of the respondents from households under $30,000 relied on clinics, emergency rooms, or outpatient departments for their primary medical care. Less than half, 45 percent, of the respondents or their spouses, including more than 40 percent of the respondents over 50, indicated that they were enrolled in a pension plan outside of Social Security. More than half of the respondents reporting incomes under $30,000 relied exclusively on social security.

Perceptions of Racial Discrimination

Nearly two-thirds, 64 percent, of the respondents said that all blacks, not just the poor, were treated unfairly by society. This opinion was held most strongly in higher-income households: 77 percent of blacks with earnings $50,000 and above, held that view, compared to 51 percent of those earning between $10,000 and $20,000. There were virtually no differences on this question between native and foreign-born blacks.

In addition, 64 percent said that racial discrimination is the cause of blacks being denied equal wages: 75 percent of those earning $50,000 or more held this view, compared to 62 percent of those earning $10,000 to $20,000. Again, there were few differences between native and foreign-born blacks.

Data from the census, the Equal Employment Opportunities Commission (EEOC), and New York City government show that blacks—notably black males—remain severely underrepresented in official and managerial jobs. These occupational disparities are reflected in the responses to the survey: Just 24 percent of those questioned held professional or managerial jobs; 72 percent of the respondents said that blacks were routinely passed over for middle-level positions; and 73 percent believe discrimination has affected their chances of obtaining executive-level positions. In both cases, more individuals from households earning $75,000 or more held these perceptions than from lower-income brackets.

When asked to identify the places where racial discrimination was most prevalent, the highest proportion of the respondents—30 percent—identified shopping areas. This reflects a long-standing complaint among black New Yorkers about being followed by clerks in stores. Another 15 percent identified restaurants, bars and other places of entertainment; 14 percent named their place of work; and 11 percent said public transportation. In each case, the perception of racial discrimination was most prevalent among the upper income groups.

Affirmative action drew heavy support: 83 percent said it was still needed in education and the workplace. As in other areas, the greatest support was among upper income households: 91 percent from households with incomes between $50,000 and $75,000 indicated that affirmative action was still needed. In other words, those black New Yorkers who, by dint of their level of income, are likely to have the most access to opportunity are most in favor of affirmative action. These findings are doubly provocative, given that New York City has never developed a strong public sector affirmative action plan and, except during David Dinkins' mayoralty in the early 1990s, has generally avoided an examination of the patterns and practices of private companies.

Relations with the Police and the Criminal Justice System

Reports by human rights groups, including Amnesty International, the city's Civilian Complaint Review Board (CCRB) and New York State's Attorney General, have documented the causes of the black community's distrust of the police: a pattern of disproportionate arrests, "stops and frisks," police brutality, and incarceration. In 1999, for example, blacks constituted one-quarter of the city's population but accounted for more than half (51 percent) of the persons "stopped," according to the New York State Attorney General's office. In 2000, blacks constituted 53 percent of all the complaints against police filed at the CCRB (CCRB January 2000), they were 51 percent of the misdemeanor and felony arrests and half the 70,000 inmates in New York State prisons (most of the inmates are from New York City).

Overall, 8 percent of the respondents said that an immediate family member was currently incarcerated or in a juvenile detention facility. In households with incomes under $10,000 the percentage increased to 10 percent. Native-born respondents were more likely to have a family member in a facility than recent immigrants. These problems are most intense for black men: 35.3 percent said that they had been arrested, even if the charges were later dismissed.

A clear majority of black New Yorkers feel apprehensive about the city's police: 56 percent said that they personally worry about being a victim of police brutality, 64 percent of black males and 51 percent of females expressed concern about potential police abuse. (see Table 2). Nearly nine out of ten percent, 89.3 percent, identified police brutality as a serious problem, including 93 percent of blacks with incomes above $30,000 (Table 3). Eighty-two percent said that police fail to treat all ethnic groups equally. Forty-three percent felt they've been stopped solely because of their race—including 65 percent of all of the males and half of the respondents from households with incomes over $30,000 (Table 4). Sixty-three percent indicated that the police abused their authority by stopping, searching or handcuffing them without reason—*including nearly three-fourths of the black men and 67 percent of the respondents from households with incomes of $30,000.* (Table 5, page 199). Forty-two percent indicated that the police used excessive force to get them to cooperate, including 46 percent of the black male respondents. (Table 6, page 199). Interestingly, those surveyed said police rarely used racially offensive language when stopping or arresting them. This matter will be explored in the conclusion.

Although fearful of the police, blacks still depend on them for protection and assistance. Slightly more than 49 percent of those surveyed said that the greatest change needed to improve their personal quality of life would be safer streets at night. Slightly more than two-thirds, 35 percent, rated the police as good in responding to calls for assistance, while 37 percent said the police response was not so good or was poor. In addition, 26 percent said that the police were good at solving crime, while 43 percent rated them not so good or poorly. On both questions, native-born blacks were more slightly pessimistic than blacks from the Caribbean or Africa.

Education

Blacks generally divided the problems in the public schools into two categories: those that are directly attributable to school administrators, and those for which the community, including parents, are responsible. Larger class sizes (23 percent), poor curriculum and standards (16 percent), poor administration (15 percent), and lack of safety (10 percent) were attributed to the failure of school leadership. These four areas accounted for nearly two-thirds, or 63.5 percent of the problems identified by the respondents, while 22 percent said troubled student home environments were responsible.

There were few differences between income groups or between native and foreign-born blacks about class size and curriculum. However, respondents from the higher-income households were more likely to cite poor administrative practices, while those from lower income households were more concerned about safety for children, and troubled home environments. A clear majority, 60 percent, says that teachers in the public schools have lower academic expectations for black students than for white students, including nearly three-fourths of the respondents in households with incomes of $75,000. The public schools' teaching corps remains predominantly white; but respondents were not asked if they felt at least some African-American teachers also had low expectations of black students.

Asked to evaluate the condition of public schools in general, 38 percent said they were about the same, one-third of the respondents indicated that the quality of the public schools had worsened over the past five years; and 23 percent felt they had improved. Respondents from lower-income households were more likely to believe that schools had improved than were those from higher-income households.

Even though blacks have serious concerns about the direction of the public schools, they do not support vouchers as a means to improve the quality of education. When asked if tax dollars should be used for vouchers, 41 percent said yes while 53 percent said that the funds should be used only for public schools. The responses differed by income levels. Nearly half, 46 percent, of the respondents from households reporting incomes of $30,000 or under supported vouchers. By contrast, only 36 percent of the respondents from households with incomes over $50,000 or more did. Vouchers are also more likely to be supported by blacks that have not completed college and by Catholics and Muslims. Many of the members of these religions are recent immigrants.

When respondents were asked about what they would do if additional money were available to improve the schools, 37 percent said they would use it to hire better-qualified teachers; 32 percent would hire additional teachers to reduce class size; and 28 percent would use it to obtain better facilities, equipment and books.

The survey also partially addressed the issue of the digital divide. Fifty-four percent of the respondents said they had a working computer at home. Not unexpectedly, over 80 percent of the upper-income households had computers but less than one-third (31 percent) of the households with incomes under $20,000.

Family Activity and Community Relations

Civic participation is problematic for black New Yorkers. They support the public schools but are not always active in parent organizations. They are deeply religious, but they do not volunteer at their churches and mosques. They perceive a brighter future for black children, but they are uncertain of how to define the problems of black males.

While there is great interest in their children and the schools, only 29 percent of the respondents said that they always attended school leadership or PTA meetings. Forty-four percent indicated that their attendance was irregular and 13 percent said that they rarely went to meetings. There were no consistent differences by income or place of origin.

Nearly 80 percent of those surveyed—84 percent of the women respondents—said religion was extremely or very important in their lives; a reality that varies little by income or place of origin. Forty-five percent also indicated that they attended religious services once a week or more. However, 61 percent said that they did not have time to volunteer in their institution activities and less than 10 percent devoted ten or more hours to their church or mosque.

Participation was also limited in other organizations. Twenty-four percent: indicated that they spent some time—usually less than five hours a week—in voluntary activities. However, 70 percent said they lacked the time for volunteer work in community organizations. There was little variation by income or immigrant status.

Regarding the future of today's black children, almost 60 percent of adults said they expected black children to be more successful than today's black adults. However, respondents from high-income households were less certain: 18 percent of those respondents from households that reported incomes of $50,000 or more said that black children might be less successful than today's adults. College graduates were also more pessimistic. Those born outside of the United States were much more optimistic about the future of black children than native-born blacks. Nearly two-thirds

(64 percent) of those respondents born in the Caribbean and almost three-fourths (73 percent) of those born in Africa thought black children would be more successful, compared to 58 percent of those born in the United States. Non-citizens were more optimistic than citizens: 65 percent to 59 percent.

Part of the apprehension about the future is rooted in concern over the problems of black males. Sixty percent or more of the respondents over 40 years old said that black males had more problems today than thirty years before: 43 percent attributed their problems to the breakdown of black families, while another 26 percent cited their own lack of motivation. Only 13 percent chose racial discrimination. Here the difference among income groups is instructive: Upper-income respondents saw the breakdown of the black family as the principal cause for their problems while those from lower-income households were more likely to say it resulted from lack of motivation.

Conclusion

The results of the survey of New York City's black civil society are a guide to understanding part of the mosaic of urban America. Because of the city's international preeminence, the findings are also a mirror of people of African descent in the new global economy.

Despite the wealth of studies and discussions about the new global economy and global cities, little attention has been given to how or whether the old patterns of racial discrimination are being maintained or altered during the current transformations. This study suggests that while New York has become the nexus for the global Diaspora of people of African descent, many of the old patterns of racial discrimination continue to target new immigrants and old residents alike.

In broader terms, the issues and challenges of this increasingly diverse urban black population suggests a need for greater introspection and a sharper critique about concepts and strategies of the past, and a more nuanced perspective of the histories and cultures of people of African descent for the future.

For example, we should revisit and expand the discussions of institutional or structural, racism that were begun in the 1960s and 1970s. The framework should have two aims: a continued examination of blacks' lack of access to good jobs, and greater attention to the policies and practices of police and other institutions—notably, the public schools—that stigmatize or exclude blacks from "mainstream" life.

There is no doubt that blacks have made considerable progress in the job market since the 1960s. However, data for New York City and most large cities continue to show a lack of access and mobility in the highest paying industries and jobs—a reality that has produced the almost universal support of blacks for strong affirmative action programs. The most explosive manifestation of this institutional racism has been the police practices of racial profiling and "stop and frisk" sweeps. While this and other surveys reveal that the arrests of blacks, particularly males, cut across all income groups—and this survey and related data on arrests also show that black women are also at risk—the burden falls heaviest on low-income and unemployed black men who are largely "contained" in certain areas. Perhaps most importantly from the perspective of changing police behavior, the survey respondents' say that police officers rarely used racial epithets even while, in their view, harassing them. This suggests as other studies and reports have documented—that negative police behavior toward blacks is less a product of individual prejudice than of institutional policies.

Secondly, in cities where the foreign-born are an increasing share of the black population, a new discourse is needed among people of African descent on strategies to address old and new problems. Bracketing the discussion only heightens the likelihood of the issues having unintended consequences. Indeed, the increasing share of foreign born blacks and other people of color

215

who can legitimately claim racial discrimination has been one of the major reasons that some analysts have raised doubts about the efficacy of affirmative action, arguing that addressing the complaints of all groups of color is too complex a task for government and the private sector (Patterson, 2001).

Third, greater attention needs to be paid to the growing problems of black women. As noted earlier, black women are at increasing risk of being arrested, stopped and searched, and their incarceration rates are increasing as well. As their high unemployment rates indicate, they also face an uncertain economic future, an uncertainty that will soon intensify, as more women are removed from welfare rolls. At the end of 2001, the five-year Temporary Assistance for Needy Families (TANF) cycle ends, and in New York, more than 40,000 women will be required to leave the program. The most recent data for 1999 indicated that blacks made up 40 percent of the TANF households. Surveys of community organizations indicate they are unprepared to deal with the women, many of them single heads of households, with limited training, and little understanding of the labor market. When Head Start providers in New York and New Jersey were asked to describe welfare reform, their most frequent responses were "confusion," "frustration," "complexity," and "fear." (Head Start Quality Improvement Center, 2000).

A fourth need the New York Urban League Survey underscores is finding ways to increase participation in black institutions and larger civic organizations.

While many contemporary discussions about the weakening of civil society may be exaggerated, this survey suggests that black civic participation is largely limited to religious institutions, and even there, the volunteerism is the work of a relatively small number of people. Participation in parental groups in the schools and community organizations is also modest because, according to those surveyed, they simply don't have time for volunteer work. The pattern in New York City's black civil society is not distinctly different from national trends, which show that the percentage of adults reporting volunteering has declined since 1989 (Nonprofit Almanac 1997) One can readily understand that while the daily pressures of urban life compound decisions about civic participation, particularly for blacks, the consequences to the status of the group of a lack of participation are enormous. Black religious and civic institutions preserve and pass on black culture, and they are a source of information about political and economic activities. Larger civic organizations are part of the balance of civil society, government, and the private sector. Without an active black civic participation, institutional racism remains unmonitored and advocacy—a major problem in New York City—lacks a black voice. Given the limited availability of computers in black households, particularly lower-income ones, there's also a danger that blacks are falling further behind in the information needed to be full citizens of the global economy.

The New York Urban League Survey and the suggestions that flow from it are in fact only a first step toward addressing the issues and needs of an increasingly complex black community. In the coming years, the Diaspora will become more diffuse, and other black communities will also see an increase in the share of their foreign-born. The income gap will also continually rise, and strain the ability of community organizations—with increasingly fewer governmental resources—to meet the needs of the poor, including a growing number of black elderly whose major resource is Social Security. Ultimately, to deal with these and other questions highlighted in the survey, greater attention needs to be given to the construction of black civil society—its institutions, leaders, and resources—and how it relates to the political community and the private sector.

Table 1. What would you say is the most important problem facing blacks in NYC today?

	All Blacks	Male	Female	< $30,000	$30,000 and above
Eco. Dev./Jobs/Unemp.	18.5%	16.1%	18.2%	20.7%	17.4%
Police	13.4%	15.7%	11.7%	11.4%	14.5%
Discrimination/Racism	12.5%	12.6%	12.4%	13.1%	11.9%
Crime/Violence	11.4%	10.0%	12.4%	10.1%	11.9%
Education	10.1%	10.7%	9.8%	6.8%	14.2%

Table 2. Is being a victim of police brutality something that you personally worry about?

	All Blacks	Male	Female	< $30,000	$30,000 and above
Yes	56.1%	63.6%	50.8%	56.8%	56.3%
No	42.2%	34.2%	47.9%	41.6%	42.8%

Table 3. Do you think police brutality is a serious problem in the New York City Police Department?

	All Blacks	Male	Female	< $30,000	$30,000 and above
Yes	89.3%	90.3%	88.5%	89.1%	92.7%
No	5.9%	5.6%	6.2%	5.2%	5.8%

Table 4. Have you ever felt that you were stopped by the police just because of your race or ethnic background?

	All Blacks	Male	Female	< $30,000	$30,000 and above
Yes	43.3%	65.4%	27.3%	39.2%	50.3%
No	56.1%	34.6%	71.6%	60.5%	48.8%

Table 5. Did the police abuse their authority as police officers, such as stopping, searching and handcuffing you without sufficient reason?

	All Blacks	Male	Female	< $30,000	$30,000 and above
Yes	63.0%	73.9%	47.9%	62.2%	67.4%
No	37.0%	26.1%	52.1%	37.8%	33.3%

Table 6. Did the police use more force than necessary to get you to cooperate?

	All Blacks	Male	Female
Yes	42.3%	46.4%	36.8%
No	56.1%	51.4%	62.5%

University, New York

References

Civil Rights Bureau, Attorney General of the State of New York, The New York City Police Department's 1999 Stop and Frisk Practices: A Report to the People of the State of New York from the Office of the Attorney General Civilian.

Complaint Review Board of New York City, Status Report, Vol.VIII, No.2.

Jarvis, C. 2000. The Effects of Welfare Reform on Head Start Programs in New York and New Jersey, Head Start Quality Improvement Center, New York.

Johnson, J. W. 1972. Black Manhattan New York Atheneum.

Nonprofit Almanac. 1997. San Francisco: Josey-Bass Publishers.

Ottley, Roi. New World Coming. 1943. Boston: Houghton Mifflin Company.

Ovington, M.W. 1911. Half A Man New York: Schocken.

Patterson, O. Race by the Numbers NYT, May 8, 2001.

Rosenwaike, I. Population History of New York Syracuse; Syracuse Press 1972.

New York Urban League Survey Methodology

This telephone poll of a random sample of 801 adults of African descent was conducted for the New York Urban League by Blum & Weprin Associates, Inc. June 5-16, 2000. The sample was based on an RDD design which draws numbers from telephone exchanges in the five boroughs of New York City, giving all phone numbers, listed and unlisted, a proportionate chance of being included. Respondents were selected randomly within the household, and then screened for race. The estimated average sample tolerance for data is $\pm$ 3.5% at the 95% confidence level. That is, the chances are about 19 out of 20 that if all black households with telephones were surveyed with the same questionnaire, the results of the complete census would not be found to deviate from the poll findings by more than 3.5 percentage points. Error for subgroups is higher.

History of the National Urban League

The National Urban League, which has played so pivotal a role in the 20th-century Freedom Movement, grew out of that spontaneous grassroots passage to freedom and opportunity that came to be called the Black Migrations. When the U.S. Supreme Court declared its approval of segregation in the 1896 *Plessy v. Ferguson* decision, the brutal system of economic, social and political oppression quickly adopted by the white South rapidly transformed what had been a trickle of African Americans northward into a flood.

Those newcomers to the North soon discovered they had not escaped racial discrimination. Excluded from all but menial jobs in the larger society, victimized by poor housing and education, and inexperienced in the ways of urban life, many lived in terrible social and economic conditions.

Still, in the degree of difference between South and North lay opportunity, and that African Americans clearly understood.

But to capitalize on that opportunity, to successfully adapt to urban life and to reduce the pervasive discrimination they faced, they would need help. That was the reason the Committee on Urban Conditions Among Negroes was established in 1910 in New York City. Central to the organization's founding were two remarkable people: Mrs. Ruth Standish Baldwin and Dr. George Edmund Haynes, who would become the committee's first executive secretary. Mrs. Baldwin, the widow of a railroad magnate and a member of one of America's oldest families, had a remarkable social conscience and was a stalwart champion of the poor and disadvantaged. Dr. Haynes, a graduate of Fisk University, Yale University and Columbia University (he was the first African American to receive a doctorate from that institution), felt a compelling need to use his training as a social worker to serve his people.

A year later, the committee merged with the Committee for the Improvement of Industrial Conditions Among Negroes in New York (founded in New York in 1906), and the National League for the Protection of Colored Women (founded in 1905) to form the National League on Urban Conditions Among Negroes. In 1920, the name was shortened to the National Urban League.

The interracial character of the League's board was set from its first days. Prof. Edwin R. A. Seligman of Columbia University, a leader in progressive social service activities in New York City, served as chairman from 1911 to 1913. Mrs. Baldwin took the post until 1915.

The fledgling organization counseled black migrants from the South, helped train black social workers and worked in various other ways to bring educational and employment opportunities to African Americans. Its research into the problems blacks faced in employment opportunities, recreation, housing, health and sanitation, and education spurred the League's quick growth. By the end of World War I the organization had 81 staff members working in 30 cities.

In 1918, Dr. Haynes was succeeded by Eugene Kinckle Jones, who would direct the agency until his retirement in 1941. Under his direction, the League significantly expanded its multifaceted campaign to crack the barriers to black employment, spurred first by the boom years of the 1920s, and then by the desperate years of the Great Depression. Efforts at reasoned persuasion were buttressed by boycotts against firms that refused to employ blacks, pressure on schools to expand vocational opportunities for young people, constant prodding of Washington officials to include blacks in New Deal recovery programs and a drive to get blacks into previously segregated labor unions.

As World War II loomed, Lester Granger, a seasoned League veteran and crusading newspaper columnist, was appointed Jones' successor.

Outspoken in his commitment to advancing opportunity for African Americans, Granger pushed tirelessly to integrate racist trade unions, and led the League's effort to support A. Philip Randolph's March on Washington Movement to fight discrimination in defense work and in the armed services. Under Granger, the League, through its own Industrial Relations Laboratory, had notable success in cracking the color bar in numerous defense plants. The nation's demand for civilian labor during the war also helped the organization press ahead with greater urgency its programs to train black youths for meaningful blue-collar employment. After the war those efforts expanded to persuading Fortune 500 companies to hold career conferences on the campuses of Negro colleges and place blacks in upper-echelon jobs.

Of equal importance to the League's own future sources of support, Granger avidly supported the organization of a volunteer auxiliary, the National Urban League Guild, which, under the leadership of Mollie Moon, became an important national force in its own right.

The explosion of the civil rights movement provoked a change for the League, personified by its new leader, Whitney M. Young, Jr., who became executive director in 1961. A social worker like his predecessors, he substantially expanded the League's fund-raising ability and, most critically, made the League a full partner in the Civil Rights movement. Indeed, although the League's tax-exempt status barred it from protest activities, it hosted at its New York headquarters the planning meetings of A. Philip Randolph, Martin Luther King, Jr., and other civil rights leaders for the 1963 March on Washington. Young also was a forceful advocate for greater government and private-sector efforts to eradicate poverty. His call for a domestic Marshall Plan, a 10-point program designed to close the huge social and economic gap between black and white Americans, significantly influenced the discussion of the Johnson administration's War on Poverty legislation.

Young's tragic death in a 1971 drowning incident off the coast of Lagos, Nigeria, brought another change in leadership. Vernon E. Jordan, Jr., formerly executive director of the United Negro College Fund, took over as the League's fifth executive director in 1972 (the title of the office was changed to president in 1977).

For the next decade, until his resignation in December 1981, Jordan skillfully guided the League to new heights of achievement. He oversaw a major expansion of its social service efforts, as the League became a significant conduit for the federal government to establish programs and deliver services to aid urban communities, and he brokered fresh initiatives in such League programs as housing, health, education and minority business development. Jordan also instituted a citizenship education program that helped increase the black vote and brought new programs to such areas as energy, the environment and nontraditional jobs for women of color. He also developed *The State of Black America* report.

In 1982, John E. Jacob, a former chief executive officer of the Washington, D.C., and San Diego affiliates who had served as executive vice president, took the reins of leadership, solidifying the League's internal structure and expanding its outreach even further.

Jacob established the Permanent Development Fund to increase the organization's financial stamina. In honor of Whitney Young, he established several programs to aid the development of those who work for and with the League: the Whitney M. Young,

Jr. Training Center, to provide training and leadership development opportunities for both staff and volunteers; the Whitney M. Young, Jr. Race Relations Program, which recognizes affiliates doing exemplary work in race relations; and the Whitney M. Young, Jr. Commemoration Ceremony, which honors and pays tribute to long-term staff and volunteers who have made extraordinary contributions to the Urban League Movement.

Jacob established the League's NULITES youth-development program and spurred the League to put new emphasis on programs to reduce teenage pregnancy, help single female heads of households, combat crime in black communities and increase voter registration.

Hugh B. Price, appointed to the League's top office in July 1994, has taken its reins at a critical moment for the League, for Black America and for the nation as a whole. A fierce, market-driven dynamic described as globalization is sweeping the world, fundamentally altering economic relations among and within countries. In the United States that dynamic is reshaping the link between the nation's citizenry and its economy, and at least for the moment, is fostering enormous uncertainty among individuals and tensions among ethnic and cultural groups.

That economic change, and the efforts of some to roll back the gains African Americans have fashioned since the 1960s, have made the League's efforts all the more necessary. Price, a lawyer by training, with extensive experience in community development and other public policy issues, has intensified the organization's work in education and youth development; in individual and community-wide economic empowerment; and in the forceful advocacy of affirmative action and the promotion of inclusion as a critical foundation for securing America's future as a multiethnic democracy.

APPENDIX | II

Index of Authors and Articles, 1987–2001

I n 1987, the National Urban League began publishing *The State of Black America* in a smaller, typeset format. By so doing, it became easier to catalog and archive the various essays by author and article name.

The 2001 edition of *The State of Black America* is the eighth to contain an index of the authors and articles since 1987. The articles have been divided by topic and are listed in the alphabetical order of their authors' names.

Reprints of the articles catalogued herein are available through the National Urban League, 120 Wall Street, New York, New York 10005; 212-558-5316.

Index of Authors and Articles
The State of Black America: 1987–2001

Business

Price, Hugh B., "Beacons in a New Millennium: Reflections on 21ˢᵗ-Century Leaders and Leadership," 2000, pp. 13–39.

Tidwell, Billy J., "Black Wealth: Facts and Fiction," 1988, pp. 193–210.

Walker, Juliet E.K., "The Future of Black Business in America: Can It Get Out of the Box?," 2000, pp. 199-226.

Diversity

Bell, Derrick, "The Elusive Quest for Racial Justice: The Chronicle of the Constitutional Contradiction," 1991, pp. 9–23.

Cobbs, Price M., "Critical Perspectives on the Psychology of Race," 1988, pp. 61–70.

Cobbs, Price M., "Valuing Diversity: The Myth and the Challenge," 1989, pp. 151–159.

Darity, William Jr., "History, Discrimination and Racial Inequality," 1999, pp. 153–166.

Watson, Bernard C., "The Demographic Revolution: Diversity in 21ˢᵗ-Century America," 1992, pp. 31–59.

Economics

Alexis, Marcus and Geraldine R. Henderson, "The Economic Base of African-American Communities: A Study of Consumption Patterns," 1994, pp. 51–82.

Bradford, William, "Black Family Wealth in the United States," 2000, pp. 103-145.

———., "Money Matters: Lending Discrimination in African-American Communities," 1993, pp. 109–134.

Burbridge, Lynn C., "Toward Economic Self-Sufficiency: Independence Without Poverty," **1993**, pp. 71–90.

Edwards, Harry, "Playoffs and Payoffs: The African-American Athlete as an Institutional Resource," **1994**, pp. 85–111.

Henderson, Lenneal J., "Blacks, Budgets, and Taxes: Assessing the Impact of Budget Deficit Reduction and Tax Reform on Blacks," **1987**, pp. 75–95.

———,"Budget and Tax Strategy: Implications for Blacks," **1990**, pp. 53–71.

———,"Public Investment for Public Good: Needs, Benefits, and Financing Options," **1992**, pp. 213–229.

Jeffries, John M., and Richard L. Schaffer, "Changes in the Labor Economy and Labor Market State of Black Americans," **1996**, pp. 12-77.

Malveaux, Julianne M., "The Parity Imperative: Civil Rights, Economic Justice, and the New American Dilemma," **1992**, pp. 281–303.

National Urban League Research Staff, "African Americans in Profile: Selected Demographic, Social and Economic Data," **1992**, pp. 309–325.

———, "The Economic Status of African Americans During the Reagan-Bush Era: Withered Opportunities, Limited Outcomes, and Uncertain Outlook," **1993**, pp. 135–200.

———, "The Economic Status of African Americans: Limited Ownership and Persistent Inequality," **1992**, pp. 61–117.

———, "The Economic Status of African Americans: 'Permanent' Poverty and Inequality," **1991**, pp. 25–75.

———, "Economic Status of Black Americans During the 1980s: A Decade of Limited Progress," **1990**, pp. 25–52.

———, "Economic Status of Black Americans," **1989**, pp. 9–39.

———, "Economic Status of Black 1987," **1988**, pp. 129–152.

————, "Economic Status of Blacks 1986," **1987**, pp. 49–73.

Tidwell, Billy J., "Economic Costs of American Racism," **1991**, pp. 219–232.

Watkins, Celeste, "The Socio-Economic Divide Among Black Americans Under 35," 2001, pp. 67-85.

Webb, Michael B., "Programs for Progress and Empowerment: The Urban League's National Education Initiative," **1993**, pp. 203-216.

Education

Allen, Walter R., "The Struggle Continues: Race, Equity and Affirmative Action in U.S. Higher Education," 2001, pp. 87-100.

Bailey, Deirdre, "School Choice: The Option of Success," 2001, pp. 101-114.

Bradford, William D., "Dollars for Deeds: Prospects and Prescriptions for African-American Financial Institutions," **1994**, pp. 31–50.

Comer, James P., Norris Haynes, and Muriel Hamilton-Leel, "School Power: A Model for Improving Black Student Achievement," **1990**, pp. 225–238.

Dilworth, Mary E. "Historically Black Colleges and Universities: Taking Care of Home," **1994**, pp. 127–151.

Edelman, Marian Wright, "Black Children In America," **1989**, pp. 63–76.

Freeman, Dr. Kimberly Edelin, "African-American Men and Women in Higher Education: 'Filling the Glass' in the New Millennium," **2000**, pp. 61–90.

Guinier, Prof. Lani, "Confirmative Action in a Multiracial Democracy," **2000**, pp. 333–364.

McBay, Shirley M. "The Condition of African American Education: Changes and Challenges," **1992**, pp. 141–156.

McKenzie, Floretta Dukes with Patricia Evans, "Education Strategies for the 90s," **1991**, pp. 95–109.

Robinson, Sharon P., "Taking Charge: An Approach to Making the Educational Problems of Blacks Comprehensible and Manageable," **1987**, pp. 31–47.

Rose, Dr. Stephanie Bell, "African-American High Achievers: Developing Talented Leaders," **2000,** pp. 41–60.

Sudarkasa, Niara, "Black Enrollment in Higher Education: The Unfulfilled Promise of Equality," **1988,** pp. 7–22.

Watson, Bernard C., with Fasaha M. Traylor, "Tomorrow's Teachers: Who Will They Be, What Will They Know?" **1988,** pp. 23–37.

Willie, Charles V., "The Future of School Desegregation," **1987,** pp. 37–47.

Wilson, Reginald, "Black Higher Education: Crisis and Promise," **1989,** pp. 121–135.

Wirschem, David, "Community Mobilization for Education in Rochester, New York: A Case Study," **1991,** pp. 243-248.

Emerging Ideas

Huggins, Sheryl, "The Rules of the Game," 2001, pp. 65-66.

Employment

Darity, William M., Jr., and Samuel L.Myers, Jr., "Racial Earnings Inequality into the 21st Century," **1992,** pp. 119–139.

Thomas, R. Roosevelt, Jr., "Managing Employee Diversity: An Assessment," **1991,** pp. 145–154.

Tidwell, Billy, J., "Parity Progress and Prospects: Racial Inequalities in Economic Well-being," **2000,** pp. 287–316.

Tidwell, Billy J., "African Americans and the 21st-Century Labor Market: Improving the Fit," **1993,** pp. 35–57.

———, "The Unemployment Experience of African Americans: Some Important Correlates and Consequences," **1990**, pp. 213–223.

———, "A Profile of the Black Unemployed," **1987**, pp. 223–237.

Families

Billingsley, Andrew, "Black Families in a Changing Society," **1987**, pp. 97–111.

———, "Understanding African-American Family Diversity," **1990**, pp. 85–108.

Hill, Robert B., "Critical Issues for Black Families by the Year 2000," **1989**, pp. 41–61.

Rawlston, Vanessa A., "The Impact of Social Security on Child Poverty," **2000**, pp. 317–331.

Stockard (Jr.), Russell L. and M. Belinda Tucker, "Young African-American Men and Women: Separate Paths?," 2001, pp. 143-159.

Thompson, Dr. Linda S. and Georgene Butler, "The Role of the Black Family in Promoting Healthy Child Development," **2000**, pp. 227–241.

Willie, Charles V. "The Black Family: Striving Toward Freedom," **1988**, pp. 71–80.

Health

Christmas, June Jackson, "The Health of African Americans: Progress Toward Healthy People 2000," **1996**, pp. 95–126.

Leffall, LaSalle D., Jr., "Health Status of Black Americans," **1990**, pp. 121–142.

McAlpine, Robert, "Toward Development of a National Drug Control Strategy," **1991,** pp. 233–241.

Nobles, Wade W., and Lawford L. Goddard "Drugs in the African-American Community: A Clear and Present Danger," and **1989**, pp. 161–181.

Primm, Beny J., "AIDS: A Special Report," **1987**, pp. 159–166.

———, "Drug Use: Special Implications for Black America," **1987**, pp. 145–158.

Housing

Calmore, John O., "To Make Wrong Right: The Necessary and Proper Aspirations of Fair Housing," **1989**, pp. 77–109.

Clay, Phillip, "Housing Opportunity: A Dream Deferred," **1990**, pp. 73–84.

James, Angela , "Black Homeownership: Housing and Black Americans Under 35," 2001, pp. 115-129.

Leigh, Wilhelmina A., "U.S. Housing Policy in 1996: The Outlook for Black Americans," **1996**, pp. 188–218.

Music

Brown, David W., "Their Characteristic Music: Thoughts on Rap Music and Hip-Hop Culture," 2001, pp. 189-201

Bynoe, Yvonne, "The Roots of Rap Music and Hip-Hop Culture: One Perspective," 2001, pp. 175-187.

Politics

Coleman, Henry A., "Interagency and Intergovernmental Coordination: New Demands for Domestic Policy Initiatives," **1992**, pp. 249–263.

Hamilton, Charles V., "On Parity and Political Empowerment," **1989**, pp. 111–120.

———, "Promoting Priorities: African-American Political Influence in the 1990s," **1993**, pp. 59–69.

Henderson, Lenneal J., "Budgets, Taxes, and Politics: Options for the African-American Community," **1991**, pp. 77–93.

Holden, Matthew, Jr., "The Rewards of Daring and the Ambiguity of Power: Perspectives on the Wilder Election of 1989," **1990**, pp. 109–120.

McHenry, Donald F., "A Changing World Order: Implications for Black America," **1991**, pp. 155–163.

Persons, Georgia A., "Blacks in State and Local Government: Progress and Constraints," **1987**, pp. 167–192.

Pinderhughes, Dianne M., "Power and Progress: African-American Politics in the New Era of Diversity," **1992**, pp. 265–280.

———, "Civil Rights and the Future of the American Presidency," **1988**, pp. 39–60.

Price, Hugh B., "Black America's Challenge: The Re-construction of Black Civil Society," 2001, pp. 13-18.

Tidwell, Billy J., "Serving the National Interest: A Marshall Plan for America," **1992**, pp. 11–30.

Williams, Eddie N., "The Evolution of Black Political Power", **2000**, pp. 91–102.

Religion

Lincoln, C. Eric, "Knowing the Black Church: What It Is and Why," **1989**, pp. 137–149.

Richardson, W. Franklyn, "Mission to Mandate: Self-Development through the Black Church," **1994**, pp. 113–126.

Smith, Dr. Drew, "The Evolving Political Priorities of African-American Churches: An Empirical View," **2000**, pp. 171–197.

Taylor, Mark V.C., "Young Adults and Religion," 2001, pp. 161-174.

Surveys

Stafford, Walter S., "The National Urban League Survey: Black America's Under-35 Generation," 2001, pp. 19-63.

Stafford, Walter S., "The New York Urban League Survey: Black New York—On Edge, But Optimistic," 2001, pp. 203-219.

Technology

Dreyfuss, Joel, "Black Americans and the Internet: The Technological Imperative," 2001, pp. 131-141.

Wilson Ernest J., III, "Technological Convergence, Media Ownership and Content Diversity," 2000, pp. 147–170.

Urban Affairs

Bates, Timothy, "The Paradox of Urban Poverty," **1996**, pp. 144–163.

Bell, Carl C., with Esther J. Jenkins,"Preventing Black Homicide," **1990**, pp. 143–155.

Bryant Solomon, Barbara, "Social Welfare Reform," **1987**, pp. 113–127.

Brown, Lee P., "Crime in the Black Community," **1988**, pp. 95–113.

Bullard, Robert D. "Urban Infrastructure: Social, Environmental, and Health Risks to African Americans," **1992**, pp.183–196.

Chambers, Julius L., "The Law and Black Americans: Retreat from Civil Rights," **1987**, pp. 15–30.

———, "Black Americans and the Courts: Has the Clock Been Turned Back Permanently?" **1990**, pp. 9–24.

Edelin, Ramona H., "Toward an African-American Agenda: An Inward Look," **1990**, pp. 173–183.

Fair, T. Willard, "Coordinated Community Empowerment: Experiences of the Urban League of Greater Miami," **1993**, pp. 217–233.

Gray, Sandra T., "Public-Private Partnerships: Prospects for America…Promise for African Americans," **1992**, pp. 231–247.

Harris, David, " 'Driving While Black' and Other African-American Crimes: The Continuing Relevance of Race to American Criminal Justice," **2000**, pp.259–285.

Henderson, Lenneal J., "African Americans in the Urban Milieu: Conditions, Trends, and Development Needs," **1994,** pp. 11–29.

Hill, Robert B., "Urban Redevelopment: Developing Effective Targeting Strategies," **1992,** pp. 197–211.

Jones, Dionne J., with Greg Harrison of the National Urban League Research Department, "Fast Facts: Comparative Views of African-American Status and Progress," **1994,** pp. 213–236.

Jones, Shirley J., "Silent Suffering: The Plight of Rural Black America," **1994,** pp.171–188.

Massey, Walter E. "Science, Technology, and Human Resources: Preparing for the 21ˢᵗ Century," **1992,** pp. 157–169.

Mendez, Jr. Garry A., "Crime Is Not a Part of Our Black Heritage: A Theoretical Essay," **1988,** pp. 211–216.

Miller, Warren F., Jr., "Developing Untapped Talent: A National Call for African-American Technologists," **1991,** pp. 111–127.

Murray, Sylvester, "Clear and Present Danger: The Decay of America's Physical Infrastructure," **1992,** pp. 171–182.

Pemberton, Gayle, "It's the Thing That Counts, Or Reflections on the Legacy of W.E.B. Du Bois," **1991,** pp. 129–143.

Pinderhughes, Dianne M., "The Case of African-Americans in the Persian Gulf: The Intersection of American Foreign and Military Policy with Domestic Employment Policy in the United States," **1991,** pp. 165–186.

Robinson, Gene S. "Television Advertising and Its Impact on Black America," **1990,** pp. 157–171.

Sawyers, Dr. Andrew and Dr. Lenneal Henderson, "Race, Space and Justice: Cities and Growth in the 21ˢᵗ Century," **2000,** pp. 243–258.

Schneider, Alvin J., "Blacks in the Military: The Victory and the Challenge," **1988**, pp. 115–128.

Stewart, James B., "Developing Black and Latino Survival Strategies: The Future of Urban Areas," **1996**, pp. 164–187.

Stone, Christopher E., "Crime and Justice in Black America," **1996**, pp. 78–94.

Tidwell, Billy J., with Monica B. Kuumba, Dionne J. Jones, and Betty C. Watson, "Fast Facts: African Americans in the 1990s," **1993**, pp. 243–265.

Wallace-Benjamin, Joan, "Organizing African-American Self-Development: The Role of Community-Based Organizations," **1994**, pp. 189–205.

Walters, Ronald, "Serving the People: African-American Leadership and the Challenge of Empowerment," **1994**, pp. 153–170.

Youth

Fulbright-Anderson, Karen,, "Developing Our Youth: What Works," **1996**, pp. 127–143.

Hare, Bruce R., "Black Youth at Risk," **1988**, pp. 81–93.

Howard, Jeff P., "The Third Movement: Developing Black Children for the 21st Century," **1993**, pp. 11–34.

McMurray, Georgia L. "Those of Broader Vision: An African-American Perspective on Teenage Pregnancy and Parenting," **1990**, pp. 195–211.

Moore, Evelyn K., "The Call: Universal Child Care," **1996,** pp. 219–244.

Williams, Terry M., and William Kornblum, "A Portrait of Youth: Coming of Age in Harlem Public Housing," **1991**, pp. 187–207.

About the Authors

WALTER R. ALLEN is a professor of sociology at the University of California at Los Angeles.

DEIRDRE BAILEY is a policy analyst for the House Committee on Appropriations for the Commonwealth of Pennsylvania.

DAVID W. BROWN is a recent graduate of Harvard Law School, and Associate Editor of *The State of Black America*.

YVONNE BYNOE is the president of Urban Think Tank, Inc., which addresses issues of concern to black Americans from the perspective of the Hip-Hop generation.

JOEL DREYFUSS, former editor of *PC Magazine*, is a senior writer for Bloomberg Markets.

SHERYL HUGGINS is a freelance editor and writer in New York City.

ANGELA D. JAMES is an assistant professor of sociology at the University of Southern California.

HUGH B. PRICE is president of the National Urban League.

WALTER W. STAFFORD is Professor of Urban Planning and Public Policy, Robert F. Wagner School of Public Service, New York University.

RUSSELL L. STOCKARD, JR. is an assistant professor of communication and business at California Lutheran University and is currently engaged in research on media and social movements in Central America.

THE REV. DR. MARK V.C. TAYLOR is the pastor of The Church of the Open Door in Brooklyn, New York, where he has developed a Council of Ministries, which specifically addresses the needs of the community for families, seniors, substance abuse, aids, prisons and evangelism.

M. BELINDA TUCKER is a professor of psychiatry and biobehavioral sciences at the University of California in Los Angeles.

CELESTE M. WATKINS is currently a Ph.D. candidate in sociology at Harvard University and a Fellow in the Harvard Multidisciplinary Program in Inequality and Social Policy.